S0-BKN-410

The Morning Comes
SINGING

The Morning Comes
SINGING

A Novel by
Kristen D. Randle

Bookcraft
Salt Lake City, Utah

Copyright © 1986 by Bookcraft, Inc.

All rights reserved. This book or any part thereof may not be
reproduced in any form whatsoever, whether by graphic,
visual, electronic, filming, microfilming, tape recording, or
any other means, without the prior written permission of
Bookcraft, Inc., except in the case of brief passages embodied
in critical reviews and articles.

Library of Congress Catalog Card Number: 86-71658
ISBN 0-88494-603-7

First Printing, 1986

Printed in the United States of America

For my parents
Jack and Jacqueline Sneed Downey

All characters in this book
are fictitious, and any resemblance
to actual persons, living or dead,
is purely coincidental.

Prologue

It is one of the grand old perversities of nature that the longer you want something—the more eagerly you anticipate it and the deeper your anxiety in the waiting—the less remarkable the thing will seem once you have finally gotten it.

Elder Soloman had spent two years dreaming about home— which is not to say his heart hadn't been in his work while he was away; you can be very seriously committed to one thing and still ache for another. He wasn't sure what he had expected, some kind of rush of—_something_—when he stepped off the plane and onto American soil again, but the only feeling that came was more of an absence of feeling, a strange sort of disappointment; and he found himself caught up in another kind of rush, the pushing of people who are trying to _get_ somewhere, and that was not specifically homelike.

The only difference between this place and the last one was that more people were speaking English than were speaking French, and Sidney gave up his expectations, letting the human tide drag him along, an insignificant, tired, and rather lost-feeling piece of flotsam.

After he had cleared customs, he stood in the midst of the noise and confusion, not sure what to do next. It was then that he saw his mother and sister. His mother had seen him, too, and she came along quickly, her arms open, an unmistakable look of relief on her face. His sister followed more slowly, allowing her mother whatever time she needed with her long-lost son.

His mother held him out at arm's length, looking him over carefully. "Hello, Claire," he said to her.

"You look terrible," his mother said, touching his very short hair with distaste, and then dismissing it with a shrug. "Paris is such a good place for food, and you come home looking like *this*. Of course, I should be grateful; it could have been worse—you could be wearing saffron robes with no hair at all." She met his look of gentle reproach with a less gentle one of her own. "Well, how would *I* know? It's been a long time since you came to visit."

He smiled at her wearily, then looked over her head at his sister who was waiting so patiently. "Hello, Courtney," he said. She smiled and with silent warmth soothed some of those parts of him that were still aching. A little of the strangeness he had been feeling dropped away.

His mother slipped her arm through his, manning the tiller for a time, and they left the crowded lobby for the crowded concourse. "You still have time to catch your luggage before they put it on the other plane," his mother said. "You're both welcome to stay for Christmas."

"Claire," Courtney said, not looking at her mother, "you know we can't do that."

"I don't know why not," her mother said, just the slightest edge of indignation creeping into her voice.

Courtney sighed. "Mother," she said, with a weariness in her voice born of crossing the same ground too many times, "first of all, his church has to release him from his mission. Technically, he's still on his mission until he can get back to California. So he has to fly back to California tonight. And then fly back to Chicago in the morning. And second—it's Dad's turn." She looked sideways at her brother.

"I don't know how you can keep track after all this time," Claire said. "Last year should have been my year, then." She looked at Sidney. "You didn't come home when it was *my* turn."

"He *couldn't*, Mother," Courtney said.

"And why couldn't you?" his mother asked him. "What kind of religion would separate a family on a holy day like that? Sidney, your father has Sally and her two children. Your father is *Jewish*. It's not like he needs to celebrate Christmas. It would only be for a few days; you could go to Chicago after. It's been two *years*."

"I can't go to Chicago after, Mother," Sidney explained patiently. He was being patient even though he knew Courtney had explained the same thing a dozen times. "I have a production

2

meeting with the band the day after New Year's. I have to be there for that. You know how important it is to me, Mother, after two years, to get back into the business. It's not like I'm in a position to keep anybody waiting."

"Well, your father still has his family," she pursued.

"And you have Eddie and Elaine, Mom," Courtney reminded her.

"Who haven't seen you for two years, either. I can understand you wouldn't be concerned about Eddie and me—just two old people. But what about Elaine? She's your half-sister, and I would like to know what I'm supposed to tell her, now? All of her friends know who you are, and that's a big thing to her. She was *very* excited that you should be coming." She stopped. "I really think you ought to stay with your family."

Sidney sighed and patted his mother's hand. "I really can't," he said. "And you have to remember that Dad is family, too." He looked down at her and smiled gently. "I'll be back, Mother. You know I will. This is just the way things have to be right now."

She looked away and then down at her watch. "You make me old when you call me Mother," she said. She straightened her lapels. "I'd like to know who decides how things *have* to be." Her two children exchanged a look. "At least Courtney used to come down and see us once in a while from school. Now you won't even do that," she said, looking at her daughter. Courtney glanced at Sidney.

"And why's that?" he asked.

"Because she's dropping out," his mother said. "And it's a waste."

"Mother," Courtney began, looking flushed. She looked at her mother's watch. "We're going to miss that connection," she warned.

"Then you'd *have* to stay," his mother said, but gave him a gentle push and started him down the concourse again. By the time they got to the gate, they had very little time. The mother kissed her two children lightly.

"Merry Christmas, Claire," Courtney said.

"Merry Christmas, Mother," Sidney said, trapping her hand for a moment.

"I don't know what your father needs with Christmas," Claire

3

said absently. "Well, have a good holiday. And Sidney, when you finish with all *this*," she waved her hand at his hair and his name tag, "come and spend a little time with your family."

"I will," he said. "You know I will."

Sidney settled himself in the seat next to his sister. She had offered him the window, but just now he had enough problems without having to look out into the void and wonder what was holding the plane up. He shoved his bag between his feet. On second thought, he pulled it out from under and dumped it on the empty aisle seat. If there was going to be an empty place on this airplane, he wanted it next to him.

"It keeps getting worse with her," Courtney said, looking out of the window. "I thought I had everything settled before you came. I'm sorry you had to go through that."

"It's okay," he said.

"You look tired," she told him.

"I'm tired," he agreed. As tired as he had ever been in his life.

"Not half what you're going to be by tomorrow night," she said. "Are you sure you have to go on to California tonight?"

He nodded, and then he dropped his head back against the seat and took a long slow breath. "It's important," he said, sitting up again. "I'll sleep on the plane. I'm hardly going to be in California long enough to know I was there. I'm not even going home. I can sleep in the plane coming back out." He patted her hand lightly. "Don't worry."

They sat in silence for a moment. And then, "So," he said, meaning to ask her about school, but she started talking again.

"It's easier in Chicago, now. Daddy has gotten mellow in the last few years, probably because of Sally, and because he's finally making some money. Actually, he's gotten to be a lot of fun. But I don't know. I don't belong there any more than I belong in New York."

"For now, you belong in school," Sidney said, not meaning to have sounded so absolute.

She turned around and looked straight at him. He thought she was going to say, "Now, don't *you* start," but she didn't. Instead, she answered what he had said. "I really don't," she said.

"I've tried. And don't think I don't understand how much you've invested in me. But, Sidney, I have to be honest. I just really don't care about my Ph.D. You have a piece of paper—so what? Does that make you happier? Does that mean you're a responsible adult? I'm not going to go back there. And don't tell me it's a waste. *You* never went to college at all, and there's nothing I can see about you that's a waste."

He wasn't so sure. "So, what are you going to do?" he asked.

Some of the fire went out of her dark eyes. "I don't know," she said, and she sat back against her seat.

He had hoped she could answer the question. Here he was, finally home, but without any *feeling* of home. Sitting beside his sister, he was sitting beside someone who could have been a stranger, considering how little he really knew about her. She said she didn't belong in New York or Chicago; he was beginning to feel as if he didn't even belong inside of himself. He thought about going back to L.A., and a dark sort of malaise began to settle over him, and if someone had asked him the question he had just asked her, he never could have answered it.

"I don't have anything I love like you do," she was saying quietly. "The music you do, it's *part* of you. It's always been that way—Sidney and music; both words the same thing. There's nothing like that for me. Except people. I love *people*. With a degree in ancient literature, the only people I'm getting to know are already dead. I wish *I* had something I love the way you love music."

"Excuse me," a voice said. Sidney looked up at the stewardess standing in the aisle beside them. "You're going to need to put your bag under the seat." She looked from one of them to the other. "You're brother and sister?" she asked. "I thought so. You look so much alike."

"Thank you," Courtney said, grinning at Sidney as the stewardess moved on.

He grimaced. "She thinks I'm pretty," he said.

Courtney laughed. "You are," she said. "You're the prettiest man I've ever seen."

"Gag!" he said. And then he looked fondly at his sister, who *was* pretty. She had the Middle Eastern mystery about her eyes, the dark, rich hair from her father, and the delicate features and coloring of her mother. The real loveliness in her face was the goodness of her, the kindness, the openness, and that was something all her own.

"How are you going to get home once you get to L.A.?" she was asking.

"Emily's had the car," he said. "She's going to leave it at the airport for me."

"She's not going to be there?"

"Her parents live in Sacramento, so she's going to drive up with her sister. I won't see her at all."

"That's sad," Courtney said, commiserating. He had to smile, even though he agreed with her. There was very little that could really upset him with this sister of his close by.

"I tell you what," he proposed on impulse. "Why don't you come down and stay with me? I'm not really looking forward to living in that house all by myself, and maybe it could give you some time to think. I think it's a good idea."

She looked thoughtful. "You may *have* something," she said.

The stewardess began to call for attention.

"So, you'll come?" he asked, a tiny bright hope stirring inside him.

One last moment of consideration. "You bet your life," she said, and, suddenly, home became more of a place.

Chicago went right by Sidney—one noisy blur of color and light and good food. He thought about it as he drove those last few interminable miles along Pacific Coast Highway on New Year's night to his little house on the beach. The Chicago days had gone by so fast that it had made him dizzy. In France the time hadn't gone so quickly.

He was exhausted, but he was hungry too—in spite of the hamburger he'd just had—and he knew he was going to be hungrier in the morning. So he stopped off at Altiri's Market, just before home. He reminded himself that he'd have no electricity and no water, so he bought a loaf of bread, some peanut butter, and some cold 7-Up.

It was a very short drive from Altiri's to his own house. When he pulled in at last, there was the old welcome home he'd nearly forgotten—the rich sound of the sand and gravel under his tires.

He stopped the car and shut down the engine, and then he sat there for a few minutes in the dark, trying to let the earth settle around him before he went up to the house.

He finally got out of the car with his tiny bag of groceries. He was thinking that Emily had taken good care of the car. It had been squeaky clean when he found it at the airport. That was just like Emily, everything clean and neat and taken care of. He decided to leave the hamburger wrappings on the floor of the car for the time being, just to make it look as if somebody lived there.

He made his way up onto the dark porch, balancing the bag on his lifted knee while he tried to single out the right key. The door opened easily after he unlocked it. He stepped inside the place and, after shutting the door behind him, was left totally in the dark. *The shutters*, he remembered. At least they were still good and tight. He blundered his way into the kitchen, by old habit reaching out for the light switch. The lights came on, blinding him. He squinted at the light switch, putting the bag of groceries down on the table, hoping the electricity hadn't somehow been left on for these last two years.

He forced himself to go back out to the car for his bags, then he hauled them into the bedroom, half heartedly opening them on the floor. He left them there, having no interest whatever in unpacking them. He went outside around the house and took the shutter off his bedroom window. He took two of the shutters off the front windows too, the ones that faced the sea, and then went back into the house and made himself a sandwich.

He didn't want the lights on in the main room. It was too empty and strange in there without his big old grand piano. He turned off the kitchen light and went back to the main room to pull the sheet off his old white cane chair. He wanted to sit just where he used to sit, here in the ambient glow of Alistairs' beach lights, his sandwich on a plate in his lap, and the 7-Up close at hand. He wanted to understand that he was finally *here*.

He was going to have to get used to the sound of the ocean again. He was going to have to get used to being alone, because Courtney wasn't going to be able to come out for a while yet.

All the furniture in the house was shrouded with sheets. He didn't like it, the empty room and the sheets. He put his sandwich down and pulled the sheets off the couch and the other chairs.

He sat down again. And he still didn't like it. The house was so silent—except for the loud sound of the surf. If it hadn't been for that, he might have lost his mind.

He closed his eyes, opened them again, and reached for his sandwich.

It had been so long since he'd been totally alone that he had to reason with himself to keep the creeping fears down. The silence of the house didn't help any. But these fears he knew he could deal with, given time. They didn't worry him.

What did worry him was another kind of silence entirely, and a rising private fear.

He finished the sandwich. There was a tiny silver clink of plate against glass table.

The structure of Sidney's thought had always been music. Some people think in words, some in pictures, some in feeling and color; Sidney had always thought in music—not only thought, but *felt* and understood. Sometimes the music he heard inside himself was someone else's music he was remembering. More often, what he heard was something all his own, a spontaneous synthesis of sound and feeling, just as loud and as real inside his head as though he were listening to someone in the very room, performing it. His earliest memories were of the music. It was the self of him. It was his heart.

Sometimes it was so loud that he couldn't hear anything else, not even with his ears.

And from the very beginning, that music had come out of his hands as talk comes out of people's mouths. From the first moment he touched a piano and understood what it was, he had had the incredible relief of *expression*, the music rising from the instrument, just the way he heard it in his head, complete, literal. He was fifteen when he'd finally understood that not *everybody* heard the kinds of things he heard, and it had always been a horrific kind of twilight zone for him in trying to imagine a mind without music in it.

It was only natural, then—not to say necessary—that he should have chosen to make music his career. He had a stage name, Halliday. Halliday had five gold records in his closet. Halliday had toured the United States a good number of times (not to mention England and the Continent) just doing what he did best, thinking out loud with his hands. He heard his music on the radio all the time. It had all ceased being novel long since.

But most important, the music preserved his precious and tenuous inner balance. He'd learned, years ago when his parents split up, that he didn't have to *need* anybody. He could build good fences out of the music, make himself whole and self-sufficient. He had been inclined over the years to suspect that he was really quite self-centered and selfish because of it. But Courtney had argued that the love of a *whole* person had no selfish need in it, and so was purer and less conditional, and anyway, she knew him very well, and selfish was certainly something he had *never* been.

That was a sister talking. At least he knew he'd never hurt anybody by taking from them more than he was prepared to give, and that was a very good thing.

Then came his mission, and the music, not really needed, had slipped away, gradually replaced by something so substantial that he hadn't even noticed the change till it had been accomplished. What carried him through the next two years was a sort of spiritual inner fabric—prayer, love, *something*—that had given him strength and direction.

Now, as he sat in his house in the dark, the one thing he was grateful for was that his father didn't own a piano. If there had been a piano in his father's Chicago house, somebody would have asked him to play it, and that would have been a terrible thing, because somewhere between France and New York, and finally, between New York and Chicago, the sweet missionary fabric had begun to fade. And nothing had come to take its place.

No music.

Nothing.

In Chicago, it hadn't seemed all that significant. He'd been able to tell himself it was only a matter of time, or, *it's just all this noise; who could hear himself think?*

But now he was home in this empty house. Nothing more had changed. In the silence here he could no longer avoid the inner silence. And he began to be afraid.

You're just tired, he told himself. *You don't know how tired you are.* But he had been tired before. A three months' tour could make you tireder than this. *So, it's the stress,* he thought. *You're just under a lot of stress.* But he'd been under stress before, too — when the family had finally broken to pieces, that had been stress, and doing albums and working with people and trying to understand Emily — these were stress, weren't they?

So, why now? Why *now,* when he needed to be so *good?* They were waiting for him, his band. They were expecting him to take up where he'd left off. He had to get on with his life, here. He had to be able to perform.

Still, there was not a sound inside of him, not in his mind, not in his hands.

Not even his thoughts would take on coherent form. And he began to be afraid that he was losing his mind.

Don't think about it, he warned himself. *Just like when you're on a high place, and you shouldn't look down. You don't think about it, and you won't panic. All you need is rest. All you need is time. Just relax. Just give yourself some time.*

He got up and took his plate into the kitchen, and he went into his room and undressed, offered a short prayer, and lay down on his bed. He listened to the ocean, and he stared at the ceiling. *This will pass,* he kept telling himself over and over, the way a mother comforts a child. *Everything is going to be all right.*

At some point in the night, he finally fell asleep.

_____ *One*

When he woke up that first morning, Sidney didn't know where he was. At first he thought it was the Rue Esperance, perhaps because the walls and the windows were so gray. But he heard the surf. And he was alone in the room.

It came to him slowly that he was home, and that this bed upon which he lay was his own.

Time to get up, his body said.

And then his mind answered, *Why?*

For a while he had no answer. And then he remembered the production meeting with the band. It was, after all, why he had left Chicago so early. He had to get up and get going so he could make a total fool of himself at the production meeting.

He sat up and swung his legs over the side of the bed. He looked around the room. *Well, this is what I wanted,* he told himself. *I wanted to be here. Now I'm here. Wonderful! What do I do now?*

On a mission, you study first. I'm not on a mission. I'm home. What did I do first thing when I used to be home?

I used to run. On the beach. Every morning, miles and miles. I used to play racquetball with Susan, too. But Susan doesn't know I'm home yet. And Susan, at this point, could undoubtedly beat my socks off.

He looked out of the window.

Fog. Who wants to run in the fog? He sighed and went through his bags, looking for running shorts—shorts and a tee shirt and some shoes. He stumbled out of his house into the clammy, chilly air and played at warming up for a moment. Then he started running.

He didn't get far. He lumbered a few good yards, then stopped, his hands on his hips, looking down at his feet, trying to get the breath back. *I used to do this? I don't want to do this,* he told himself. *Who can run in this sand? And I'll probably get pneumonia out here, anyway.*

So he turned around and lumbered back to his house. At least he ran the whole way up to the house, even up onto the porch. He even kept his feet moving while he unlocked the door. It made him feel better, knowing he had given it his best shot.

He went into his bedroom and sat down on the bed, puffing, pulling his shoes off. He threw his shoes into the closet, one after the other, sand flying everywhere. *It wasn't like I didn't exercise in France,* he thought. *It's got to be the sand.*

He took a shower. He turned on the radio in the bathroom, trying to get a feel for what was happening on the air waves these days. He got dressed—jeans, sweatshirt, tweed jacket, white boat shoes, the Sidney-at-home uniform—and he felt a little better. He made himself a peanut butter sandwich, ate it, all the time listening to the radio and thinking that Top 40 sure hadn't gone very far. Then he brushed his teeth.

Just before he left the bathroom, he looked at himself. He looked at his own face, into his own eyes. It was then that the panic hit him. He didn't recognize himself. He didn't know who he was anymore. He didn't feel comfortable in his own house, he couldn't run on the sand, after today he didn't have the faintest idea what he was going to do with himself, and today they were going to expect him to play something at the studio; that was something he utterly could *not* do.

Suddenly, the silence of the house, the emptiness of it, his total failure to fill it up, terrified him. Grabbing his checkbook and his car keys, he fled, locking the doors behind him—mostly to keep the nothing that was inside, inside.

_____ _Two_

It was an unfortunate circumstance that brought Emily through the doors of Broadstreet Recording Studios that day. Kinsey, Emily's sister, was _supposed_ to be taking her to the airport to catch a plane. Now, Kinsey—whose intentions were always good—had always had a rather tenuous understanding of time and reality, and Emily, an intelligent and very practical being who nonetheless could easily be reduced to a state of near-hysteria by the simple act of having to catch an airplane, was finding herself growing less and less comfortable with every passing moment.

Just when Emily had finally felt sure she would get to the plane in time, Kinsey announced the necessity of a very short side trip—_very_ short—exceedingly short—momentary at the longest—because C.J., her husband the guitarist, had forgotten something very important—his very favorite pick or something—which had to be delivered to him _now,_ while he was still at the studio. Emily could only look at her watch and resign herself. There was time. There was a little time.

It was encouraging when Kinsey pulled in against what was a yellow curb, just in front of the studio. But when Kinsey shut down the car's engine and, removing the baby from her safety seat, disappeared, baby and all into the building, Emily was no longer encouraged. You don't take a baby along, Emily thought darkly, when you're just dropping something off, not when there's a perfectly responsible adult sitting there in the car with the baby, wanting to catch an airplane.

The only explanation for it was that Kinsey, in the heat of the moment, had forgotten all about Emily, all about the airplane, all about Emily's last semester at school and her degree and her future sense of accomplishment, not to mention the roommate who would be waiting around at the airport in vain.

The fact of the matter was that Emily wanted, more than she had wanted anything in her young life, to finish school. She had an irrational terror that something would come along that could keep her from doing it, and she was fiercely protective of her rights in that regard.

The longer Emily sat there in the car, the more deep her suspicion became that her sister had indeed forgotten. She finally got herself out of the car and went looking for the errant Kinsey.

Emily knew the studio very well; she'd worked there the past two summers as substitute receptionist. There were a hundred places Kinsey could have been. Marge wasn't sitting at the front desk, so Emily simply began opening doors, getting more and more desperate as the time went by and Kinsey was still nowhere to be found.

Finally, as she stopped outside one of the tiny production rooms, Emily heard some music. It was Graham's voice, and where Graham was, C.J. and Kinsey must be. Emily pulled the door open. There was a man sitting in a chair, Kinsey's baby in his lap, but no Kinsey to be seen anywhere. A line of cold apprehension dropped right down Emily's throat into her stomach.

And then the man turned and looked at her. She looked straight into his face for a moment before she looked away, and she was just thinking he had a lot of nerve, staring at her that way, when something about the eyes caught at her and made her look at him again.

She never would have known him. It was Sidney sitting there with the baby in his lap. It was Sidney, but he was very thin, and his face was different. It was his hair, maybe—she had forgotten about the missionary hair. The short hair changed his face. That had to be it. The way he was looking at her was kind of the same, enough the same. The little ball of panic that had been sitting in her middle expanded itself and spread all over, down into her legs, out into her arms. She had to lean against the door frame.

"Why didn't you call me?" was the first thing he said to her, and his voice was wrong, too.

"Well . . . why aren't you in Chicago?" she asked him, and her voice wasn't any better.

"I came back for this," he said. "I would have been back before now if I'd known you were going to be here." Slightly accusatory, more hurt, mostly at a loss, steadily holding on to the baby.

She was still looking at him, shaking her head slowly. "We just got back," she said, explaining, defending, not saying what she meant because there really wasn't time for that. And he wasn't saying what he meant either because this wasn't the place for it.

"You could have called," he said again, looking as if this wasn't the way he wanted things to go.

"It was after midnight," she said. "I thought you were in Chicago."

"C.J. didn't tell you about this," he said, as if it were impossible she could have been ignorant.

"No," she said.

He nodded slowly, a little vacantly. "Can you sit down?" he asked, definitely casual now, but pulling at her.

"I've got to catch my plane," she said, panic blossoming to something just short of tears. "I'm late. I came in here to find Kinsey."

"She'll be back," he said, not letting go of her. This was the nightmare; he was going to end up making her stay here—just that look in his eyes could do it, that sad-dog pull. She was going to end up missing her plane and then she'd never get back to school. It was like a trap, this room and those eyes. "This is my last semester, Sid," she pleaded. If he understood what this meant to her, maybe he'd stop the pulling.

"It's been two years," he said.

"I'm graduating magna cum laude if this semester goes right," she told him desperately. It wasn't supposed to be like this after two years, all off balance and wrong like this.

"You know what that means? It means I already have ten major companies offering me *jobs,* Sidney. *Good* ones. I can do anything I want to do."

15

"That's nice," he said absently.

She looked at him. "I'm going to work here for Cap again this summer," she added, watching his face. But he didn't understand what she was trying to tell him.

"I don't think you're listening," she said.

Somebody brushed her shoulder coming into the room. Emily moved to get out of the way.

"What are you doing, Emily?" Kinsey said, gathering up the baby. "This girl is going to miss her plane. You want to tell me why you're not in the car like I told you?" Kinsey balanced the baby on one arm and grabbed her sister with the free hand, turning her, shoving her out into the hall.

Emily was looking at him back over her shoulder, willingly—unwillingly, helpless under Kinsey's onslaught. And he just sat there, empty-armed.

"Four months," Kinsey called back over her shoulder. "Call her tonight."

The sad smile of a man lost was the last thing she saw of him as the door closed behind her.

"You should have stayed in the car," she said, shaking Emily ever so slightly as they left.

Emily got into the car, angry now. "So, why'd you take so long, Kinsey?" she said.

"It couldn't have been that bad," Kinsey said.

"It was." Emily's eyes were tearing up—not a lot, just more than she wanted them to. They started up the ramp to the freeway.

"I expected to have to pry you two apart," Kinsey said, checking her rearview mirror and pulling out into the traffic for all the world as if she had been born and bred on the freeway.

Emily was shaking her head. "I wish it were that easy," she said. "I'd never have been able to leave there if it'd been like that."

"You make your own trouble," Kinsey told her. "I don't know what you want."

"I know you think I've been a total jerk about this whole thing. I don't even want to talk about this anymore, Kinsey. I really don't. Okay, I made a big mistake about marrying

Warren. At least I didn't *do* it." She shuddered, and Kinsey agreed silently.

"But I am a passably intelligent person. And if you want to get down to it, I knew a lot more about Warren than I know about Sid. I loved Sid from the beginning. But I'm not going to throw out my entire education on the chance that things *might* work out this time. I just wish I hadn't run into him like that. That was the *worst*."

She checked her watch again.

"You could have told me he was going to be in there," Emily said quietly.

"I didn't know."

"C.J. knew."

"He probably didn't even think about it."

"I could've at least said 'How was your mission?' or 'It's good to see you' or something. I didn't even recognize him at first."

"I think he's lost weight," Kinsey said, and turned off for the airport.

Emily shook her head again to herself. "It hurt me to look at him," she said. "He looked so lost. I wish I'd been warmer."

"Sid's a big boy," Kinsey said.

"I don't know," Emily said. "I just wish I could have talked to him."

Sidney made a fist and beat it very lightly on the arm of the chair. Then he sighed. *I could have done without that little interchange,* he thought. He looked down at his shaking hands. It made him angry, this whole business of Emily. Her letters had been such lies, warm and candid and kind. It was a different woman who had spoken to him just now, and that difference frustrated him, angered him. He balled up that whole set of anxieties and put them away where he hoped he wouldn't have to feel them. Just now, he had other things on his mind.

He moved restlessly in the chair, unable to concentrate on the music he was supposed to be listening to. He shut the recorder off, fished the cassette up out of it, and, sticking that in his pocket, made his way back to the main control room, where the rest of the band was working.

Two years really hadn't made much difference in any of them. Chris was still the impossible person he'd always been: crude, foul-mouthed, overbearing, and insensitive—a great drummer, but rather a lousy human being. Being in the same room with him today had been like being rebaptized into the world. He was evidently working on his fourth marriage, and Sidney found himself sympathizing with the poor woman.

Sidney had never been able to figure out what had drawn Chris and Graham, the real forces behind this outfit, together. Graham was the antithesis of Chris. He was easily the sweetest man Sidney had ever known—quiet, kind, a gentleman in every sense of the word. His songs were beautiful, even the fast ones. Graham's voice was his instrument, and he'd always known how to use it.

As Sidney came through the door into the control room, he heard them laughing. Tall, black, South African Nee, the bass player, a gentleman in his own enigmatic way, was sitting back against the wall on one side, C.J. on the other. C.J. smiled at Sidney; there was that sort of family familiarity between them.

"Don't you ever change that shirt?" Sidney asked. C.J. was wearing the same C.F. Martin tee shirt he'd had on two-and-a-half years ago in this same room.

"That's his skin," Nee said, his voice low and mellow and pleasant.

Chris came into the room and immediately mounted the console dais, putting himself in the producer's seat with the absent air of someone who is used to being there. Graham stood in the doorway, just watching.

"Where's Cap?" Sidney asked. His nerve was slipping.

"He's still back in the lounge, I think," Graham said.

"When's he going to get something back there worth drinking?" Chris grumbled.

"When are *you* going to learn to appreciate Hansen's Natural Grapefruit?" C.J. asked him. Nee held up his own can of it and grinned.

"Get wild," Chris said sourly.

Graham laughed. Cap, the owner of the studio and the chief engineer, came into the room and Sidney's stomach tightened. It was time to get down to business.

Cap stood behind the console, beaming at Sidney. He put his arms out and asked, "Have I changed much?"

"You didn't grow any hair while I was gone," Sidney ventured.

Cap laughed. "I didn't lose any weight, either."

"Okay," Chris said. "So. What did you think of the tunes? Those are the charts you've got there?" He pointed at the pile of manuscript paper Sidney had in his lap now.

Sidney swallowed and looked down at the charts. "Yeah," he said. "Okay," Chris said, waiting for a reaction.

Sidney sighed. "They're pretty good tunes, most of them," Sidney said, stalling. He looked up and found that Graham was watching him. Graham smiled.

"So, you're going to play us something," Chris said rather than asked. It was the thing they all expected—that Sidney would already have the complete production in mind. It's the way they had always done things. Sidney listens to the tunes— out pops the production. Except, not this time.

Now he looked up at them, clearing his throat. "I want to explain something to you gentlemen." He spoke very carefully, trying to choose the right words. The rest of his professional life rode on these few moments. "I haven't really played much in the last two years. Not this kind of thing." He patted the top chart. "I just got in last night," he looked at his watch, "about twelve hours ago, actually. My piano's still in storage. I don't even have a synthesizer to my name anymore."

He looked at Graham. "I'm not sure I can do this," he said.

Chris was tapping the eraser of his pencil on the producer's desk. He and Graham exchanged a long look.

Graham looked at Sidney. "Are you telling us you don't want to do it?" he asked.

Sidney ran his hand over the top chart. "I've been asking myself that." He looked up at them. "If you want to take a chance on me, I want to do it. I'll give you my best, whatever I've got."

Graham nodded. Chris was watching Graham. Nee and C.J. and Cap were silent.

"I'm going to tell you something, kid," Graham said, "and I want you to take this very seriously. We've been in the business a long time. And we've never seen anybody with a gift for music like the one you've got. You're a tremendous musician. Two years outside of it, and anybody could get slow. We've got lots of time. Chris is going to be in Canada in June. We can't do anything till then, anyway. Nobody's going to push you. You can just take your time. You've got to understand, Sid—it's more than that. We're friends, you know?"

There was a murmur of assent. Two years hadn't done anything to toughen up Sidney's sensibilities; he was not far from tears at the moment.

"The truth is," Chris said, "you've always been pretty much a pain in the neck." He gave Sidney a half smile. "But you turn out gold records, and that's the bottom line."

"Gosh, thanks," Sidney said, half smiling himself. He stood up and patted the mess of charts into a more or less uniform pile on his arm. "Okay," he said. "I'll call you." He looked at Graham. "We'll get together in a couple of weeks. It's good to see you guys." And then he was gone.

Nobody said anything for a little time. Then Chris shook his head and flipped the pencil at the door. "You give a man religion, and you take away his—"

"Watch yourself," Graham admonished.

"Well, it's true," Chris said, angry now. "The guy used to have some *life* to him at least."

"He's just a little disoriented," Cap said, fiddling with his console. He had a little screwdriver out and was poking at one of the modules. "He'll get over it."

"Every other word I said, the man *flinched*," Chris pointed out.

"We all do that," Nee said.

Chris threw up his hands. "I don't know how I ever got tied up with you guys," he said. "It's like an old ladies' sewing circle." He threw himself back in the chair. "But I'm telling you. It's the religion that's doing it to him. He's not going to come through. He hasn't got it anymore. You could see that."

C.J. had been sitting there, one leg widely crossed over the other, elbow on knee, chin on fist, listening. Now he shifted, digging a pick out of one of his pockets. "I don't think you can blame it on the religion," he said. He knocked a piece of lint off the pick.

"That's because you're one of them," Chris said. He held back on the disdain.

"You've got to consider," Nee said thoughtfully, "Sidney is probably more of an artist than any of the rest of us. Except, perhaps, C.J.," he added. "People like that tend to be more affected by things, more sensitive. Except C.J." He smiled. "Stress," he suggested. "Emotion. Fatigue."

"He's just disoriented," Cap said again. "I'm telling you, he'll get over it. They all do. I went through it myself once, remember."

"What do you mean, you went through it yourself?" Chris asked, rounding on him.

Cap said very plainly, very clearly, "I'm one of *them* too."

Chris looked at him blankly. And then some understanding began to creep in. He held up one finger and pointed it at Cap, narrowing his eyes. "Suddenly a lot of things are making a lot of sense around here," Chris said.

"Poor Chris is always the last to know," Nee said, grinning.

"I have better things to do than hang around with a bunch of religious ascetics," Chris said, standing. He looked at Cap. "I can't believe they let you into their church, you old pirate," he said.

"So, there's always hope for *you* then, isn't there? Get out of here before I start charging you double time," Cap told him. "And that goes for the rest of you. I've got a bunch of synthesizers coming in here in an hour, and I'm not set up for it yet." They stood up. "Call me," he said, smiling, "when you're ready to make some music."

_____ *Three*

Sidney sat in his car and studied his house. He was not inclined to go back in there—not by himself. He knew he was being irrational, but there wasn't much he could do about the way he felt.

The house looked weather-beaten, which was just as it should have been; it was that kind of house. He was going to have to wash the windows, especially the ones in the main room that looked out over the ocean. Shutters hadn't kept out the silt or the sand. And he was going to have to work on the shingles because the roof was in pretty bad shape. Maybe he could do a little painting and sealing. The little veranda needed a good sweeping. And the house would be a lot less strange once the piano was back.

He began to warm up to it, all this work. The empty places in his mind didn't seem as empty for a moment. If he could just keep busy, maybe everything would settle down; maybe he'd look around, and everything would be normal again.

So, all right, he told himself. *Go get some groceries. Call the phone company from Altiri's and get your phone hooked up, and then call somebody and get the piano back in here.*

So that's what he did. And the best part of it was coming home from Altiri's, because there was somebody on his front porch when he pulled in, somebody who turned when she heard his tires in the gravel, somebody who waved and yelled as he threw open his door.

"Hi!" he said, bone-pleased to see her. "Hey, Susan!" He'd been afraid she might have cut her hair while he was gone, but she hadn't. It still hung, dark and heavy as midnight, down her back. She put something down on the porch, danced down the steps, and met him half way with her arms out. It was by far the

nicest hug he'd had in a long time. He even got a little kiss out of
it.

All the attention made for a tiny bit of euphoria that bounced
around the vacant insides of him for a while, like an echo in a dry
canyon. She helped him carry the groceries in.

"Don't step on the pie," she warned him. Of course, she'd
brought a pie. He looked down at it over the tops of his grocery
bags. It looked wonderful. Of *course* it looked wonderful.

"I haven't even had any lunch," he said mournfully.

She put her sacks down on the kitchen table. "Well, you *look*
like you've spent the last two years in some third-world country.
Didn't you *eat*?" She didn't even wait for an answer. Pointing at a
chair with that unequivocating air of female authority, she began
to unpack his groceries. *This* was what he had hoped for the
moment he saw her. In the kitchen Susan's hands were magic.

But there were other parts of her that were just as interesting,
he couldn't help thinking as he watched her move around the
room. Her presence made the room warm and took the strange-
ness of it away.

"Oh," she said, "go get the pie." Cheerful now he did as he
was told, and by the time he got back with it there was something
in a pan on the stove and she was setting a place for him at the
table. He stood there with the pie in his hand, looking down at
the single, forlorn place mat.

"Aren't you going to eat with me?" he asked.

She looked at him with disgust. "Have I *ever* eaten *anything*
at this time of the afternoon?" she demanded. Of course not.
How could he have been so *stupid*? But he looked at her so piti-
fully that she finally gave in, just as he'd known she would.

"I can't say no to you," she grumbled, and she set another
place.

It was only chili she was making, chili basically out of a can.
But, oh, what she *did* to it!

"You don't know how lonely this place is," he told her. She
was stirring the chili. The way she did it, it looked like a little
dance.

"Oh, yes I do," she said. "I checked in once in a while. It's a
sad place without you here, Sonny."

Now things were beginning to make sense. "You didn't come in here and clean," he said.

"I came in here to borrow your books," she said, dignified and admitting nothing. "You *said* for me to go ahead and borrow them if I wanted. If I had to dust things off so I could see what I was doing, what else could I do?"

"Wench," he said happily. "Does the phone work, too?"

"Did you try it?" she asked. He got up and went out into the main room. "It works," he called. Then he came back in and sat down. She put the bowls down and poured the chili into them. The steam rose up and warmed his face.

"So, how've you been?" he asked.

She handed him a spoon. She shrugged. It had not been the right question; or, maybe it was.

"Not so good?" he said.

She shrugged again and sat down.

"You know," she said, stirring at her chili—there was hardly enough to stir in her bowl—"you say this place is lonely." She looked at him. "It really isn't. Every time I came in here, there was . . . like . . . a part of *you* here." She shrugged. "I like it in here. There are lonelier places. You know, the whole time you were gone, I kept thinking about you and Emily. I kept wondering, how does that girl keep him on the line that way? I mean, you never . . ." She gestured slightly. He understood her.

"Never," he said.

She shook her head. "I don't understand you," she said. "How old are you? Twenty-six, now? Sidney, do you really think that's *healthy?*"

The way he was feeling at the moment, he was inclined to think she had a point.

"But you never lose interest in her. She keeps you at arm's length all these years, and there you are, still faithful dog Trey. I don't understand it. As far as I can see, she never gave you anything but trouble. What kind of a hold does she have on you? Because whatever she's got, I could use some of it."

"Anything she's got, you've got," he said.

Susan laughed. "Evidently not." She lifted her spoon thoughtfully. "You know, even after all this time, I'm still a little in love with you. Maybe we just all want what we can't have."

"That's a sad thought," he said.

"Sad but true," she said, and then she took a drink. "You remember Cory? my friend Cory?"

"The one who was staying at your place," Sidney said flatly.

"The one who was *living* with me," she corrected him. "Off and on for the last four years." She sighed. "I wish I knew how to make him stay." She looked at Sidney. "The truth of the matter is, I'm really kind of a faithful dog Trey myself, and I'm getting tired of this. Sidney, I'm going to admit something to you; and if you ever tell anybody, I'm going to kill you. You know what I want? I really want to get married. You should have something in your life you can depend on. Something besides your instrument. I don't want to be married to my cello. I want a *person,* and I want a person like *you.* So, how do you do that?"

He laughed, embarrassed. "I don't know, Susan." He stuck his spoon into his bowl. "It's not like I'm having such terrific success myself." He studied her for a moment. "All right. I'm going to tell you something my mother used to say to Courtney. But you are *not* going to like it."

"Okay," she said, tilting her chin at him.

"Nobody's going to buy the cow if he can get the milk free."

She regarded him with distaste. "How insulting," she said.

"Well?" he said. He didn't have to tell her that what she was already doing wasn't working.

"*Cow,*" she said ruefully. She got up and went to the fridge. As he watched her cross the room, he couldn't imagine why he wasn't in love with her. But what could he do? That was the way it was. "So," she said, turning, "did you convert the heathen French?"

It was worse after she left for rehearsal that evening. He tried to fill the house up with noise, but he could stand only so much of the radio. When he knew he was going to have to go to bed at last, his hands started to sweat. He stood by the windows in the front room for a while, watching the surf slide up the gray beach, and he kept as still as he could, just in case there was any faint thing to be heard. All in vain.

The only thing that came to him was a memory of Emily, some night out on the beach before it all fell apart. That nice companionable feeling, good conversation. And kissing. There hadn't been a whole lot of that even then. There didn't seem to be much hope for the future now, either.

So, he was lonely. On top of everything else, he was lonely. He felt it through his whole body. Not a nice way to feel in the dark, alone. Lonely and scared.

What if it never comes back? he was asking himself. *What if nothing ever happens to me again?* He put his forehead against the cold window glass. *What if I'm trapped in here for the rest of my life?*

He learned something that night. He found out that if you leave the lamp on, the darkness isn't so loud. If you leave the lamp on, it's almost easy to fall asleep.

The second morning wasn't as confusing. The ocean had him back now; his body remembered the rhythm. He looked out of the window. Fog, again. Gray air, gray water, gray sand. He knew exactly where he was. He sighed. It began to rain.

He got up and began to unpack his bags—clothes in all the old places, scriptures on the night table, brushes of all sorts in the bathroom. He hated unpacking; it had always been the worst part of a tour, and it wasn't cheering him up any now.

He was about to heave the empty suitcases up onto the heap of stuff in the extra bedroom when he stopped for a moment, realizing that Courtney was going to need a place to sleep.

"Aha!" he said, pushing the door open and turning on the light. Here was enough work to drown any sorrow. Days' worth, weeks' worth—just finding a place for all this junk. "The room is *filthy,*" he pronounced, thoroughly satisfied with it.

He spent the day on that room. He left the light on that night and slept reasonably well. The next day the rain persisted. Sidney went into the extra room, and *he* persisted. By that afternoon both the room and the weary world were washed clean, again rendered useful to mankind.

The rain let up, and the days began to flow into one another —long nights with the lamp on, up in the morning for a run, back home to find something to do. The shingles were delivered. Sidney went out and bought a new tool belt and a great many useful tools. He spent long hours on the roof getting splinters and making a minor mess of his hands. His mother would have given him what for about it, too, and so would Graham. But Sidney couldn't really see what difference stiff hands were going to make at this point. Anyway, busy hands are happy hands, and happy hands don't have time to remember how scared they are.

Susan dropped by now and again. Once he saw her running along the beach with some guy, chummy-chummy, and she gave Sidney a covert thumbs-up. Sidney sighed.

Every day he worked hard. And for a while, the busyness seemed sufficient. He knew that in the end he was going to come hard up against the fact that nothing was changing; the gift was still gone—maybe forever—and he was going to have to get on with the rest of his life, regardless. He planned to deal with that someday. But not now; he didn't think his poor distressed brain had the courage.

The first thing he did every morning was turn off his lamp, because if he forgot and left it on all day the bulb might blow, and then how would he ever go to sleep again?

Then things got worse.

There was the night when Susan showed up on his porch looking like the very shadow of gloom itself. Seeing her, he understood that she didn't want to come inside, and he understood that he was supposed to come outside. What he did not understand then was that she was really very upset.

He found that out when he sat down beside her in the sand, down towards the water. She was crying, and that really did him in. That's when he made the worst mistake, the easiest mistake. Susan was a Tough Little Soldier, and here she was, giving up. He had to console her. What else could he have done?

"Cory can't use a dry cow," she said bitterly. Sidney put his arm around her. She allowed him. She leaned against him, and then, with very little prompting on his part, she turned and buried her face in his shoulder. He rested his cheek against her hair.

She drew away slightly, looking up at him. He saw embarrassment—maybe shame—in her face. What he felt might have been compassion. He thought it was empathy. He kissed her forehead, gentling her; then her eye. And, before he had known he was going to do it, he kissed her on the mouth.

She shouldn't have let him do it. But she did. She did better than that; suddenly, she was kissing him back, and his nervous system went up like a field of dry grass in August, just that fast, just that hot.

They got a better hold on each other, and they kissed again. In a moment of lucidity he realized what he was doing, and he pulled himself away, staring at her through the dark.

They sat there for a moment in silence. Then she said, "*You* kissed me."

"I know," he said. He was feeling sick.

"You didn't mean it," she said, her voice flat.

It wasn't easy for him to say it. "No. Not the way it happened." *Why don't you just go ahead and kick her in the face?* he asked himself.

"I want you to sleep with me," she said.

It chilled him. "No, you don't," he said.

"I do," she said. She was trying to hurt somebody.

"We wouldn't be friends anymore," he said. It was the only thing that had come to him.

"I don't care," she told him.

He was still staring at her, unable to get this clear in his mind. "I think you do," he said.

"Excuse me," she said, and she got up.

He caught her hand, needing to explain to her how brittle he was, how empty and scared. But the right words weren't available, and the only thing between them was the silence. She shook off his hand, and she walked away.

"I'm sorry," he said, not loud enough that she could hear it. But that was fine, just fine, because the words were so inane.

He sat there alone on the chilly beach for a long time. Then he said to himself, *Come on, old son, old liar, old jerk. You've got to get to bed, man. You've got church tomorrow. Time to get on in there and be afraid of the dark, now.*

He stood up slowly and brushed the sand away.

It would have been a lot easier just to junk everything, but he couldn't figure out how to do that.

_____Four

Sidney stood in the back of the chapel, awkward and self-aware, almost a stranger. The old bishop was gone. Most of the faces he didn't recognize. Other people were moving around as if they were part of the place. Sidney was not part of the place.

Old Miri Krause was still sitting where she had always sat, there in the back where she could see everybody come in. That was comfortable. It was a little continuity. She was a nice old lady, and he'd been her home teacher for some months before his mission. She'd always been nice to him. Some people had found her interest in them an intrusion; he had never felt that way himself. Now he considered speaking to her, but she was busy with somebody else. He wouldn't have known what to say to her, and anyway she was bound to remember that he had played the piano. She'd always gone out of her way to compliment him on his playing, and that was the last thing in the world he wanted to talk about at the moment.

There were few other familiar faces. Sooner or later, if he stood there long enough, somebody was going to notice him and want to shake his hand and make him talk; this anonymity he was enjoying was a luxury, and he knew it. Next week, they would know he'd returned. Next week, they'd make him stand behind the podium and report on his mission. Maybe next week, he could stand that. But for now, he found himself a place to sit, a nice, empty pew in the middle of the room, about half-way back. He felt safe enough there for the time being. He closed his eyes and listened to the prelude music.

Somebody slid in past him and sat down on the other side. Sidney kept his eyes closed until he couldn't stand it anymore. He opened them and reached for a hymnal, sneaking a look at the newcomer, and finding that the newcomer, a sandy-haired young man, quite lanky and pleasant looking, had been sneaking a look at him. Sidney stuck out his hand philosophically.

"Calvin Arrington," the man said. His voice was a lovely baritone.

"Sidney Soloman," Sidney said. They nodded at each other and smiled. Then the meeting started. As things progressed from meeting to meeting, it became evident that Calvin had taken Sidney under his wing. Calvin, very much with the air of someone who wore a suit for a living, graciously led the way, shepherding Sidney along, introducing him to people, educating him as to changes in the building, and, in the end, volunteering him for an elders quorum assignment.

And that was fine with Sidney. But he made sure that Calvin got his due. He made Calvin promise to help him finish the shingles on the roof. It all worked out very nicely; for a little while Calvin had been a bit of a panacea. And then it was time to go home.

Miri Krause caught Sidney on the way out, looking him over with those bright, shrewd old eyes of hers. Sure enough, she talked about his music. He sidestepped it as kindly and as smoothly as he could, but the damage had been done, and the fears came crowding back.

Sidney went home and made some spaghetti. He left a dish of it on Susan's front porch with a poor little bumbling note stuck in it, and he hoped for the best.

"Okay," Calvin said, pulling on his work gloves and squinting up at the roof. "So, what do you pay?"

It was not the best day for working on a roof. There was a storm coming in from the northwest; the breeze was fresh off the ocean and it was fairly chilly and unpleasant.

"I've got leftover spaghetti," Sidney said. He hefted a bundle of shakes and climbed the ladder with them.

Calvin nodded. "Good enough," he said. "I haven't eaten that well for weeks."

Some hours later, toward noon, Susan showed up. Sidney

was loading up his pouch with nails when he saw her standing down by the foot of the ladder. It gave him a bit of a start. He hoped she hadn't come to tell him what a jerk he was; he knew that well enough already. Whatever it was that had brought her, he missed her, and he needed the air cleared between them.

As he was climbing down the ladder to her she called to him. He turned and saw that she was holding up a picnic hamper. The wind was whipping her hair around into her face. She drew it back with one hand and squinted up at him.

He took the hamper from her as he dropped down the two last rungs to the ground.

"I couldn't believe it when I saw you up there," she said. "You must be out of your mind, in this weather."

"Susan," he said, incapable of the small talk till he'd settled the rest of it, "I'm really sorry about the other night—"

She gestured shortly, stopping him. "I know," she said. "So am I. We're both a little . . . ," she tipped her hand back and forth, "these days. It's all right. Let's not do it again." He was tempted to plant a kiss right on her forehead, but he forbore.

"You're going to make yourself sick out here," she called after him as he climbed roofwards again.

He grinned down at her from the roof and waved. "Thanks," he called. She shook her head and took herself home.

They ate what she'd made up for them, and then they worked for a little longer. But it was growing unbearably unpleasant up there, and Calvin finally pointed out the gray sheets of rain that were driving in from off the sea. So they packed everything up, battening down the hatches, and retired to the relative warmth and brightness of the house.

"Make yourself at home," Sidney told Calvin as they came in. Calvin slid out of his jacket and unclipped his tool belt. He dropped both of them on the floor by the door and blew on his hands. "I'm going to have some Sleepy Time," Sidney said, heading for the kitchen. "You want some?"

"Sure," Calvin said. He didn't want to track anything on the nice wooden floor, so he took off his shoes and padded after Sidney, taking stock of the surroundings as he went. He dropped into a kitchen chair and stretched out his feet over the heat register. "That's the biggest piano I've ever seen," he said. "It's got to be twelve feet long."

"Nine," Sidney said. "I just got it back in here. I had it in storage while I was on my mission." He turned the heat up under the water.

"Whew," Calvin said. "I'd hate to have to move that sucker." He looked down at his feet. "How come you went on a mission so late? If you don't mind my asking."

"It's okay," Sidney told him, popping a couple of pieces of bread into the toaster. "I joined the Church about three years ago. You remember Bishop Bearclaugh?"

Calvin laughed. "Oh, yes. He was a relentless fella. He used to take the quorum apart over home teaching. So he got you, huh?"

"Yea, well, when he says to you, 'I *feel* like you should go,' what are you going to say?" He dropped an herbal tea bag into each of two mugs. "I hate the way herbs smell," he said.

"There *are* times when you can tell a bishop no," Calvin said thoughtfully.

"There are?" Sidney said. He poured the steaming water over the tea bags. The rain was coming down on the house now, spattering against the windows in the main room.

"I don't know. Maybe there aren't." Calvin accepted one of the mugs. The toast popped up. Sidney handed Calvin a spoon and buttered the toast.

"You have a girl?" Calvin asked, stirring his tea slowly.

"Not really," Sidney said. "I thought I had one . . ."

"She got married on you," Calvin guessed.

"In a way." Sidney handed him a piece of the toast. "She's in *school*. She put me on hold. But I don't really have time for that."

"The modern woman," Calvin said, lifting his mug. Sidney sat down across the table from Calvin. "Really," he said, accepting the commiseration.

"What do you do?" Sidney asked.

"Besides roofs?" Calvin asked. He took another sip of the hot herbs and put the mug down on the table. "I'm a lawyer."

"You're kidding," Sidney said. Then he remembered the beautiful cut of Calvin's three-piece suit. "You must be a very serious man," he said.

Calvin gave him a half-smile. "What do you do?" he asked.

Sidney looked down into his mug. "I play piano," he said, then took a drink.

"For a living?" Calvin asked.

"Yeah," Sidney said.

"What do you do? You play in clubs or something?"

"Mostly studio work," Sidney said. "Sometimes I do some touring."

"You can make a living doing that?" Calvin asked.

"You can if you're good enough," Sidney said, thinking to himself, *and that's the germinal question.*

"You play with a band?"

"I play for Doc Halliday."

"Hmmm," Calvin said. "So you work with the big boys." He nodded thoughtfully. "I thought Doc Halliday was a keyboard man."

"He is," Sidney said.

"But you play keyboards for him."

"Yep."

"Doesn't he play for himself?" Calvin asked.

"Yep. He always plays for himself." Sidney took another drink of the tea.

"You're perplexing me. The only way I can see that you could play *for* him if he plays for *himself* is if you are him. He. Which you are not. Are you?"

"Yep."

"Yep, what?"

"Yep, I'm him. He. I am he." Sidney took a deep drink of the tea. He put the mug down on the table.

"I was having such a nice time," Calvin said. He looked Sidney over for a long, sober moment. He held his mug as if to take a drink from it, and then he added, "and then you had to go and get weird on me."

"It's the truth," Sidney said.

"I believe a man's delusions are a man's own business," Calvin said.

Sidney made an exasperated sound. "Okay," he said. He got up and left the room. Calvin could hear drawers being pulled rapidly open and shut in the other room, papers rustling, lots of papers falling.

"Okay," Sidney said, stalking back into the room with the air of a man satisfied. "The lawyer wants evidence. Fine. Here's a copy of my DBA—both names on it. You see, 'Doing business as Doc Halliday' "—he was squinting at the paper and pointing. "I assume you know how to read legal forms," he said. "*And*—a copy of my financial statement. Also with two names." He opened the refrigerator and pulled out the bowl of spaghetti.

Calvin was studying the forms. He looked up at Sidney.

"You see?" Sidney said. He put the bowl of spaghetti in the microwave.

Calvin looked down at the financial statement again, nodding slowly. "Actually, I believed you in the first place," he said. "I am assuming, if the numbers I see here are correct—"

"Which they are," Sidney said.

"*If* they are, I have been grossly taken advantage of." He eyed the microwave with a touch of wistfulness. "It wasn't very pleasant up there on the roof," he said, again with the half-smile. "You could be paying better. I should have held out for pizza."

_____Five

Some of Courtney's earliest memories were of her parents' divorce. She had just turned ten at the time, and it was the end of life as it had been. An ugly time for all of them, at least it had finally left their house quiet.

Courtney, ever an almost instinctive believer in personal accountability, had never believed in shouldering guilt about things for which she had no legitimate responsibility. The divorce, then, except for the disruption in the stability of her life, had not hurt her as badly as it might have.

Her mother, on the other hand, seemed to care nothing at all for such things, preferring to delegate her guilt. Her children were the obvious candidates, and if Courtney had refused to be moved by her mother's remonstrations on everything from the filthy house to the thanklessness of parenthood, Sidney had been very receptive.

Courtney could remember the empty look he wore in those days. He was a lost soul, torn completely apart along with the family. Every time his mother walked out of the door—shopping, club meeting, church, whatever—he _knew_ she wasn't coming back. He developed a sort of gentle aloofness, immersing himself in his music.

Sidney was two years older than his sister, but she, swallowing up her unhappiness in compassion, had been the one to offer comfort to him. Now they were friends. That didn't mean she understood him. She didn't. She understood his sweetness and his honor and his honesty, but she didn't understand what went on in his mind, and she was utterly lost when it came to his music.

What she hoped to find in Los Angeles, she didn't know. Primarily she wanted to put Cornell and all her old life behind her so that she could start something new. The fact was that she was deeply impressed by her brother's involvement in his new faith. Whether she could share his beliefs, she didn't know. That she wanted to bask in the intensity of his commitment, she was sure. She had been tired and heavy and directionless for too long.

He picked her up at the airport, very much the charming person she had expected, the same outfit—tee shirt and sports jacket, blue jeans, and white canvas shoes—she'd always known. As she began to talk to him, though, and as she looked closer, she realized that his eyes were a touch hollow and he didn't look so healthy.

"What's up?" she asked him while they waited for her luggage. "Aren't you sleeping?"

He hedged before he finally said, "Not real well."

She tried to get him to talk about it but he seemed preoccupied, and she gave it up for a while. As they drove down the freeway she tried again, but all to no avail. "*Sidney,*" she said finally, "I don't think you're listening to me."

He looked slightly startled and vaguely guilty. "I'm sorry," he said. "What were you saying?"

"I'm asking you now if you've been eating right."

He laughed. "You'd have to define 'right.' "

"Ah," she said, mentally rolling up her sleeves. "And how long have you been wearing that tee shirt?"

"Why?" he asked, glancing down worriedly at the underarm seam of his jacket.

She shook her finger at him. "You haven't been taking care of yourself," she accused.

"Good enough," he argued. He lapsed into silence, and she sat back against her seat beginning to glow with satisfaction. By the time he'd parked his car outside the house, she was a happy woman. He opened the car door for her and went around back for the bags. She got out of the car and stood there, gazing out at the bright, pure blue of the sky and smelling that briny ocean smell. Then she saw the house, that poor little old place just crying out for somebody's attention. Suddenly, she was bristling with *direction*. Sid came around with the bags, and she planted a loud kiss on his cheek. He looked at her as if he thought she might be crazy, but that was just fine. She had come home.

As the days went by, Courtney found projects enough for her energy — replacing the big ferns that had once swung so lyrically in the front windows, scouring floors and stoves and bathrooms and walls. It was playing house at its best; she didn't *have* to do any of it.

Life fell easily into a pleasant routine — awake with the fresh morning sun, a short shower, a brief tour around the honey-oak bedroom Sidney had put together for her, straightening things up. The only wrench in the works would have been Sidney with his dark preoccupation and his silence, except that worrying over him was the greatest delight she had. It never occurred to her in the beginning that something might be seriously wrong with him. As the days went on, however, and things didn't change, her play-worry sobered up into a sort of mild-to-serious concern. He was not a happy man, but she could not figure out why.

When Susan came around to Sidney's again she wasn't expecting Courtney to answer the door. She hadn't expected to see Courtney at all. That he hadn't told her Courtney was coming didn't really surprise her; Sidney wasn't talking about much of anything or anybody anymore.

But here she was, standing on the porch, facing Sidney's sister. Susan was shy with other women. She'd met Courtney once, years ago, but that didn't make things any easier. What saved her was that Courtney was not shy with anybody. Before Susan could feel the pains of awkward small talk, Courtney had her sitting in the front room, talking away as if they were old friends.

Courtney asked her about the orchestra, about how it felt to be a cellist, about how long she'd lived down here on the beach. In the end, of course, it was Sidney they talked about.

"He's been moping around here like the ghost of Hamlet, or something," Susan said. "Do you know what it is?"

"No," Courtney admitted.

"Alistairs next door asked me yesterday why they don't hear Sidney practicing anymore. I haven't heard him playing note one on that thing since he got it back in here." Susan looked at the piano suspiciously. "Is there some *thing* in his religion about playing piano? Like Lent. Do Mormons have Lent?"

"I don't think so," Courtney said, smiling. "There sure isn't much life in him lately, is there? I mean, he's working hard. He just never says anything."

"You don't think he could be lovesick, do you?" Susan asked. "Not over Emily. Selfish little—You know about Emily."

"I know something about Emily," Courtney said, "but Sidney hasn't said anything about her. Which doesn't really tell us much, I guess. I don't know. He's just being so strange. I was kind of hoping *you* knew something."

"Not me," Susan said. "Even when he talks, I get confused. But it'd better not be Emily. I'd like to poke her one in her sweet little eye."

Courtney's face was thoughtful. "Well, if that is it, you just have to remember, she can't help the way Sidney feels. We all have to make our own choices. I think I feel sorry for her."

Susan considered Courtney for a moment. "I don't think *I* can do that," she said. But she was fairly sure that Courtney actually could.

"Don't look at me like that, Susan," Courtney said. "It's just easier not to be angry." She frowned. "So you haven't heard him play, either." She shook her head. "That's really not good. I don't know what it means to other people, but the piano's always been sort of a release for Sidney. He feels things, and then he plays them, and then he's free of them if he needs to be. He's always been like that." She leaned towards Susan slightly. "Does he look bad to you?" she asked.

"Awful," Susan said.

Courtney nodded, her own maternal impulses justified. "Okay—well. May I get you anything?" she asked, suddenly aware of her responsibilities as woman of the house.

"You didn't bring any coffee with you, did you?" Susan asked hopefully.

"No," Courtney said.

"And of course, *he* didn't think of it," Susan said.

"I gave it up about a year ago anyway. The caffeine was beginning to get to me." Courtney moved towards the kitchen. She stopped, her hand on the big piano, and turned.

"Is he good at this?" she asked. "I mean, as a *musician.* I mean, I know *I* think he is. But really, professionally? You see, I don't really know that much about him, his life out here."

"Courtney," Susan said, quietly, "he's a Mozart. He's a Gershwin. They don't come any better."

Courtney nodded again. She laughed. "You know, all through school his grades were awful. People were telling my mother he'd never make anything of himself." She looked down at the piano. "We could never even afford to give him lessons. Sometimes I wonder what he would have done if we hadn't had a piano."

"I've heard him play a million times. I've even played on sessions he was conducting. I'm telling you. They don't come any better."

Courtney went on into the kitchen and Susan followed her. The front door opened, and they heard Sidney come in. He came into the kitchen, rubbing his cheek with the back of his hand. There was sawdust in his hair, and there were flecks of paint on his face and on his shirt.

"Hi," he said. He grinned at them. He went straight to the refrigerator and rifled around in it until he found a Hansen's Natural. He closed the refrigerator door and leaned back against it, popping open the can. He took one deep drink out of it and wiped his forehead with the back of his arm.

"You've been talking about me," he said conversationally.

They stole a look at each other—the guilty two.

"That's nice. You have something in common." He took another drink.

"If it's nice to have worry in common," Susan said.

He regarded her. "Don't worry about me," he said. "I'll be just fine." He pushed himself away from the refrigerator and left the room.

"He's a liar," Susan said after she heard the front door close behind him.

"I don't know," Courtney said. "Whatever it is, I'm beginning to think it's *something*." She opened the cupboard. "I *know* it's not drugs."

Susan shook her head in agreement.

"He's not in financial trouble. I know that, because I took over his bookkeeping. I don't think it's Emily," she said. "Well . . . ," she smiled at Susan, "for the time being, I guess all we can do is keep him from doing himself damage."

"That may not be so easy," Susan said. "He's a very creative person."

"I know," Courtney said smiling. "So, we're just going to have to be more creative than he is."

_____ *Six*

There were times when Emily wondered if what she was doing was really worth it. The long evenings at the library (who could study in an apartment where five other girls were living?), the pressure, the whole schmeer. One thing was sure: on this particular evening she should *not* have let old Carson Bean take her anywhere, not even to the library. First of all, he didn't really go up there to study; he went up there to *socialize*. Second of all, he had *ideas*. His ideas were nothing like Emily's.

When she finally got home, she was tired and cross, and as she walked down the sidewalk to the metal stairway, shoes crunching the late ice, she wondered why on earth she had decided to live with five girls who would undoubtedly be up *talking* half the night.

She opened the front door and warm yellow light spilled out into the chilly air. The only person in evidence was Kim, Emily's own Roommate-Most-Likely-to-Irritate. Kim was the kind of girl who wore french braids and played guitar—tall, really quite beautiful, and seemingly effortlessly successful at whatever she tried. Emily was a worker. Kim did well enough to please herself without putting a strain on her own energy.

Emily dropped her books heavily onto the couch, looking at the novel-engrossed Kim. *Life,* she thought, *is not fair.*

Kim looked up from her book. "Your friend called from California," Kim said. Emily wasn't Kim's favorite roommate, either.

"What friend?" Emily asked, moving her books and dropping herself onto the couch.

"Your *friend*. Your *boy*friend."

"Sidney?" Emily asked, surprised. On second thought she wondered why she should be surprised. "Did you talk to him?"

Kim smiled at her a little oddly. "Yes," she said. "*Cute* man. You know, he has a very nice voice. It's kind of sexy, actually."

"Well, what did you tell him?" Emily asked, a little impatient.

"I told him that you were up at the library with Carson Bean." Kim smiled again.

"Why'd you tell him *that*?" Emily said, fielding a rush of awful dismay.

"Because that's where you *were*," Kim pointed out. "I told him it was no big thing. I told him you only had eyes for him. Okay?"

"I'd better call him back," Emily said, standing up.

"I wouldn't. He said he was going to bed."

"When did he call?" Emily asked.

"Mmmm . . . ," Kim looked at her watch, "about nine? About nine."

"And he was going to bed?" Emily asked. Life wasn't getting any better.

"We talked for a while," Kim said, and then she went back to her book.

"Wait a minute," Emily said, not fielding a stab of pure jealousy. "What do you mean, you talked for a while?"

Kim looked at her icily. She put the book down in her lap. "When he called here, he was somewhat depressed. He needed to talk to somebody."

"He doesn't even know you," Emily said, jealousy gone to anger. Anger somewhat under control.

"Emily, sometimes it's a lot easier to talk to somebody who *doesn't* know you. And he needed to talk. So, we talked."

Emily sat back down.

"What did you talk about?" she asked.

Kim's eyes seemed to flash a bit at the question. Emily thought, *You want to see flash, you just keep this up, lady.*

"I asked him if his mission went okay. He said he used to think so. He said he wasn't so sure anymore. It seems that things aren't going very well for him right now, and he was wondering if maybe he hadn't worked quite as hard as he could have on his mission."

"He couldn't believe that," Emily said.

"He seemed to," Kim said. "And he asked me if I'd ever been so frustrated over something I couldn't control that it made me crazy." She was looking at Emily very directly. "I told him, sure —taxes and the price of gasoline do it to me all the time. So we felt better because we were both frustrated."

"That's nice and counterproductive," Emily said. She wanted to say something intelligent and biting to this girl, but she was too tired. And anyway, her brain didn't work that way.

"Well, we can't all be productive, can we?" Kim said. She picked up her book again. "Anyway, he's an interesting man. It was the most stimulating conversation I've had in a long time."

"Okay, well," Emily said, standing up, bristling all over, "next time somebody calls for me, you just take the number and tell them I'll call them back, okay?"

Kim looked up at her serenely. "Next time he calls," she said, "he may not be calling for you."

Emily wanted to pick up the lamp and whack Kim one with it. Or, she thought, *maybe I should just heave these horrible old boring books at her, one by one.* Instead, she gathered up her books and left the room in dignified silence. She hated Kim. She hated Sidney. She *hated* old Carson Bean. And she hated school. But most of all, most definitely, intensely, and passionately, she hated herself.

She went to bed, swearing that she would never go to the library again, that she'd rather die than marry Sid, that she was not going to finish school, and that some day, she would punch Kim right in that snooty nose of hers. It was a long time that night before she could fall asleep.

_____ *Seven*

On the first Sunday morning, Courtney woke, as she always did these days, to the sound of the shower. Sunlight cascaded through her window, spilling happily onto the wooden floor. She lay quietly in her bed, looking at a print that Sidney had chosen for her, a Maxfield Parrish with a translucent sky. She had spent so little time in this room, but it was more home to her now than any other place she knew.

The shower went off. Courtney sighed and began a long, thorough stretch. She intended to stay where she was this morning as long as she could. There was a funny little glass robin sitting on the table right next to the bed. She could see the room reflected in his fat sides. She could hear her brother in the other room, opening and shutting drawers and doors, but she couldn't bring herself to the point of rising.

At last there came the inevitable knock on the door.

"Good morning," she sang, and the door opened. Sidney, dressed for church, hair still slightly damp, leaned into the room.

"You're going to church with me?" he asked.

"Of course," she said.

"If you want breakfast, you'd better get up," he said. He looked at his watch. "We've got forty-five minutes."

"Get out," she said. "Fry eggs."

He smiled. "It's so nice to have a woman in the house."

It was almost music, going to church with someone who actually belonged to him; Sidney had never done it before. He was watching her as she entered the chapel with him, his dark-eyed sister, his pretty sister, and he was proud.

Miri Krause was sitting in the pew just beyond the door. She caught sight of them and beckoned. Sidney led his sister over and introduced the two of them. Of course, they hit it off instantly. Miri had one thing to say to him: "Do come up and see me, dear. I have something I'd like very much to show you." And then she and Courtney both forgot him.

In the end, he got tired of trying to stay out of the heavy traffic in the aisle, and he suggested that they just *sit* there, for goodness' sake, as the pew beside Sister Krause *was* empty. So they did, the two women conversing away in some private, female manner that left Sidney sitting there all by himself, a hungry man amidst plenty.

Then came Calvin. Calvin saw Courtney long before he saw Sidney. Sidney *saw* Calvin seeing Courtney. Then as Calvin was shaking hands with Sister Krause (without taking his eyes off Courtney for more than a moment), he saw Sidney. He did a double take. "This is my *sister*," Sidney said, and it came out more as though Calvin should watch his step than that he should enjoy her acquaintance.

Calvin raised his eyebrows at Sidney, and Sidney subsided into his collar and tie, a disgruntled man. Calvin took Courtney's hand solemnly. "You have a name?" he asked. She laughed and gave it to him. "Very suitable," he said, and then he sat down next to Sidney. "You sly dog," he said. "You might have mentioned that you had a sister, but you *never* told me she was a Courtney."

"Well, that was interesting," Courtney said. She sighed, looking out of her side of the car at the fine green ocean.

"It didn't make you feel weird or anything?" he asked, just checking.

"No," she said. "The people at your church are very nice people. And I didn't hear anything that I thought was particularly strange."

He sighed.

"Why?" she asked, "Were you afraid I would?"

He smiled. "No. I just don't know how you feel about all of this."

She looked at him. "I feel fine about this," she said. "Why shouldn't I? I'm open to new ideas. This church is part of you, and that's what I came here for, to be with you. You can't be *with* somebody if you don't at least try to understand how they think, and it seems to me that a person's religion is a fairly significant part of how they think. So, don't worry. I feel fine. It's not like I'm going to get *offended*. I don't have enough opinions about this kind of thing that I could get offended. Okay?"

"Okay," he said. He seemed to her a little brighter this morning, a little more aware of what was going on.

"I asked Calvin to dinner," she said.

"Really," he said. He pulled into the little driveway.

"He looked so hungry," she said.

"He always looks hungry," he told her.

She laughed. "And he's so solemn."

"Not really," Sidney said.

"I love this ocean," Courtney murmured. Sidney got out of the car and came around to fetch her. "You know," she said, "I'm glad I came."

Later, while Courtney was in the kitchen alone, Calvin and Sidney draped themselves over a couple of chairs in the main room. They had been thrust out of the kitchen earlier, protesting and offering to help all the way.

"She's playing house," Sidney explained. "If she ever decides to get married, she won't be like that anymore. I know. Susan tells me things about women."

Calvin grunted. "What kind of a cook is she?" he asked. "I don't want to get my expectations up without some probable cause."

"Just go ahead and let them go," Sidney told him, sighing. "She's celebrating that I got called into the Sunday School presidency today. She doesn't understand these things." He sighed again and added sadly, "I'm starving."

"She isn't LDS, I take it?" Calvin asked. The water was running in the kitchen, and Courtney was singing to herself.

"No," Sidney said. "None of my family but me. I thought she did pretty well this morning."

"She did very well," Calvin agreed. "She just didn't know some of the moves. You've been discussing things with her, I presume?"

"Not really," Sidney said. "It's harder with your own family."

"You should be talking to her," Calvin said.

"I know."

The water went off.

"Gray day," Sidney said. He was losing the morning's energy. "So," he said to Calvin, "you're going to help me paint shutters this week?"

"Am I?" Calvin asked.

"A man who comes to dinner in this house becomes family." Sidney cast a glance at the kitchen. Good smells were coming from there. "Unless you've changed your mind and you'd rather not eat."

"When do we paint?" Calvin asked.

"Thursday."

"Thursday. Afternoon. I've got a brief to finish in the morning."

"Fine," Sidney said.

Calvin was studying the twisting cane that made up the arm of his chair. "You ought to talk to her," he said again.

Sidney looked at him. "Will you knock it off?" he said. "Calvin, I'll *do* it. But right now I have enough problems of my own without *talking* to somebody."

Calvin studied him soberly.

"I'm tired," Sidney said. "And I don't think I have things straight in my brain anymore."

"So, you're having a little problem adjusting," Calvin said.

"Adjusting," Sidney said blankly.

"From your mission," Calvin said.

"From my mission," Sidney repeated. "Adjusting from my mission?"

"It's like culture shock," Calvin said. "Everybody goes through it. One day you're on a schedule and you have a companion and you know what you're going to wear and what you're going to do and who you're supposed to be working for, and you're aching to be home. The next day, you're home. One day you can't get within arm's length of anybody female; the next day people wonder why you aren't married yet. It can really mess you up."

"Everybody goes through that?" Sidney said.

"Well, some more than others. When I came home, I came home to parents and brothers and sisters and aunts and uncles, and started school three days later, and I was too busy to feel much shock." He was still looking at Sidney. "What you came back into was more or less a vacuum, I think."

Sidney nodded slowly.

"It's natural," Calvin said, shrugging. "And then you've got woman trouble besides." He looked at Sidney and smiled. "Man —you should be a basket case."

Sidney smiled.

"Okay, you guys," Courtney called. "Somebody get in here and set the table."

"You," Sidney said to Calvin.

"I don't know where you keep the silverware," Calvin protested, nevertheless rising.

"Come on," Courtney said, leaning out of the kitchen, her hands, encased in bright mitts, holding something that steamed.

"I thought *you* were going to do everything," Sidney said to her.

"Within reason," she said. "Get going."

It was late when Calvin finally left, late and dark and comfortable in the little house. Sidney stood at the front window in the main room, quite full and very sleepy. The lights were out in the room and he could see the luminescent waves rolling up onto the beach. For this one moment there was quiet, rather than roaring silence, in Sidney's mind.

Courtney turned the light off in the kitchen, came in, and settled herself on the couch.

"Calvin finished the chicken," she said.

"It was very good," he told her. "Thank you."

And then there was a silence between them.

"Sidney," she said, sounding unsure of herself. He had forgotten she was there. Now he noticed the inquiry in her voice, and he sighed.

"Is something wrong?"

Is something wrong, he thought. *I'm losing my mind, and she wants to know what's wrong.*

"Yes," he said. "There's something wrong. But it's with me, not with you. It's not something that you need to worry about." It suddenly struck him that what he was saying might be coming across too harshly. "There are just some things I have to work out in my own mind. It has nothing to do with you." He turned towards her. "You are the only sane thing in my life at the moment," he said. "And I'm very glad that you're glad you came. Does that make sense?"

"Yes," she said. "It does. Thank you."

There was another silence.

"I want you to understand," she said, "that I love you. And I'm always here for you. If you need to talk, I swear, I'll listen. Sometimes love is all you need to make the difference."

"Thank you," he said. He was ashamed that he couldn't have said something with more meaning in it.

"Good night, Sidney," she said.

He stood there by the window for a time after that, listening to the sounds of her busyness—shutting down the kitchen, brushing her teeth, all of it—the sounds of life. He thought about what she'd said about love, and he wondered if it had actually meant anything.

Eight

"Courtney, I thought you told me Sidney's grades were awful," Susan called from the living room. She was leaning back against the piano, surveying the vast array of books that lined the wall between the kitchen and the bedroom hall. There were more books over and around his desk.

"They were," Courtney said. She was cleaning out the refrigerator. She came to the doorway, wiping her hands on a towel and using the back of one wrist to push her hair out of her eyes.

"I wonder why," Susan murmured.

"He just didn't care," Courtney said.

"Have you ever really looked at this library? I must have read nearly every one of these while he was gone. I never even thought about it before—the kind of books these are. Look at this." She pointed out something on one of the shelves.

Calvin, carrying a filthy shutter, came in through the front door and headed for the kitchen.

"Sidney hasn't read any of those," he told Susan. "He just keeps them there for the effect."

Susan glared at him, and Courtney put a hand in the middle of his chest, checking his forward progression. "And where do you think you're taking _that_?" Courtney demanded.

"I've got to wash this shutter off," he said, sidestepping her.

"There's a hose outside," she said, sidestepping to intercept. He slipped by her and disappeared into the kitchen. She sighed and shook her head, and then she grinned at Susan, who was grinning back.

"Okay, so?" Courtney said.

"Okay, look—we've got Dostoyevsky . . . Hemingway . . . Shakespeare, Eliot, Thurber—Goldman? Oh, yeah—have you read _The Princess Bride_ yet? He'll make you do it. Okay—

Dickens, Dumas, Twain, Scott, Nibley—who's Nibley? McConkie. Who's—oh, these are Mormon books here. Poetry, Cervantes, Burroughs, Bradbury—Here's Beowulf."

"You're kidding," Courtney said. "Let me see." She put her hand out and Susan put the book into it, still looking over titles. "Here's another one I haven't read," Susan announced, pulling something off the shelf.

Sidney came in, little splatters of paint all over him.

Courtney held the book up. "Why do you have this?" she asked.

"What is it?" he asked, squinting. He was putting some nails in his mouth, heading for a piece of trim that had come loose around the window.

"Beowulf," she told him. "The original."

"I read the Donaldson," he said, pulling the hammer out of his tool belt.

"That's not a bad translation." She slipped the book back into its place. "Why would you be reading Beowulf?" she wondered.

"What are you *doing*?" Sidney asked, standing where he could see into the kitchen.

"Get lost." Calvin's voice sounded further away than it should have, as if he had turned his back to Sidney. Courtney leaned back, justifiably suspicious, and peered into the kitchen.

"That's one of my best towels," she said indignantly.

"So, I can get you another one," Calvin said.

"What's going on?" Susan asked, laughing.

"I read it because,"—Sidney was placing a nail high on the moulding—"my sister was an Old English specialist at Cornell, and I wanted to find out what was so exciting." He tapped the nail a couple of times lightly, then gave it a good whack.

"And did you find out?" Courtney asked.

"Nope," he said, grinning at her back over his shoulder, his teeth still clenched around the nails. Calvin laughed.

"Courtney says you did foul in school," Susan said.

Sidney took the nails out of his mouth, dropping all but one into a pouch on his belt. "Right-o," he agreed.

"Why?" Susan said, still incredulous. "I would have thought you were magna cum laude or something."

"I could never get into the system, I guess," he said, picking up a stray nail. "Anyway, I had better things to do. I knew what I wanted, and it wasn't there." He put in the last nail. "Anyway, I did okay."

Courtney grimaced. "You did *not* do okay."

"But you *read*," Susan said.

"I always read," he said. "That's all I did, the whole time I was in school—read and played the piano. I never had time for anything else." He stuck his head into the kitchen and called cheerfully. "Will you *come on*?"

"You go ahead," Calvin said, his mouth evidently full of something. "I found something in here."

Courtney's eyes went wide. "What did you find?" she asked.

"Nothing," Calvin called.

"Get out of there, Calvin," Courtney said, making a dive for the kitchen. There was the sound of a short scuffle, laced with some poorly suppressed laughter. "That was *supposed* to be for *tonight*," she was saying. "*CALvin!*"

Sidney had lost track of time. With Courtney there to take care of the logistics, all he had to do was keep moving, keep busy, keep his mind occupied with the complex demands of simple things. He was keeping his demons largely at bay in this way, more or less one step ahead of them. The secret, he found, was not to think about anything.

He knew when the next Sabbath day was coming up because the night before Courtney had made a big deal about pressing his good Sunday shirt. And she surprised him that night. She said, "Susan wants to go tomorrow."

"Where?" he asked, wondering how much of a conversation he might have missed.

"To *church*, Sidney," she said.

"You're kidding."

She looked at him, the bottle of spray starch in her hand. "What's the big deal?" she wanted to know.

"I don't know. She never wanted to go to church before," he said.

"Well, she's going," Courtney said.

"Does she know what to wear?" he asked, decidedly dubious about Susan's sense of judgment in matters such as these.

"She *knows*," Courtney said.

And, as it turned out, Susan apparently *did* know. She was waiting out by the car for them the next morning, standing in the fresh sunlight, and the utter correctness of her knowledge was pleasantly disturbing to him. "Hey," he said. "You're hiding your knees."

"Shut up," she told him.

Of course, Susan got along with Miri just as well as Courtney had, so they all had to sit in the back of the chapel again. And, of course, Calvin managed to get himself another invitation to dinner. It was the beginning of a ritual, actually. Every Sunday after that Courtney planned for four people, but she always made Calvin beg for his invite; she got a lot of pleasure out of working his imagination.

It was always the same: there were two who cooked and two who did not. The two who did not were not even allowed to do the dishes, so they always resigned themselves to their privileged state and lolled about all over the furniture, winking knowingly at each other about how things would be around here *after* anybody got married, and complaining about how much they'd eaten.

On the first Sunday they spent all together, Calvin introduced to the girls the concept of family home evening, offering to come over the next night and educate them about it, seeing that Sidney himself had been remiss in the matter. It meant another dinner invitation. And it became another institution.

On Wednesdays the two girls took to visiting with Miri Krause at her little house up on the cliff. On Thursdays Susan and Calvin came over for games, Trivial Pursuit more often than anything, and Sidney's quiet little house was suddenly a very busy place.

And that was all right with Sidney, because you can't keep working all the time, and people mean noise and diversion and talk, and when there were other people talking (Susan and Calvin were both good talkers), Sidney didn't have to do it. Besides, he had had enough lucid moments in the past weeks to have noticed that he wasn't being what you'd call great company for his sister, but he hadn't known what to do about it, except to feel unpleasantly guilty. This family that seemed to be evolving was the perfect thing. Courtney had friends, he had another fine fortress against his fears, and everything was rosy. Until he had to go to bed at night.

Every night he tried to keep Courtney up late, hoping to keep her talking. But it never did any good; sooner or later, everyone went away and left him alone in the dark. He didn't like to be alone in the front room. Every time he looked at the piano, he felt as if he'd lost a lover, and every time he *looked* at it, his hands got clammy, and he began to get that cold, tight feeling in his mind.

If you just manage to keep busy enough, he told himself, *you might not ever have to admit something's wrong. And if you keep humming to yourself, you'll never even notice how quiet your life is.*

_____ *Nine*

It was a gorgeous spring morning, balmy and compelling. Sidney had gone wandering inland, hungry for new green things, up over the highway, and up further to the cliff's edge. He hadn't really been *going* anywhere, but he ended up on Miri Krause's front porch.

She had a beautiful little cottage, a storybook place at the end of a little private lane. You had to walk under a rose-draped arch to get into the yard. Once you were there, you could stand and watch the ocean and the beach below, the clean breeze in your face and the bright clouds very near. It was a tremendous beach property, and it was worth a fortune, modest as it was.

With his hands in his pockets, and no very clear idea of what he was going to do or say once she opened the door, Sidney stood in the yellow sunlight with the breeze sifting through his hair. He hadn't heard the door open, so it startled him when she spoke.

"I'm so glad you came," she said. He couldn't really say anything to that; he wasn't at all sure why he had come. He just smiled at her, and she took his arm, pointing out all the things that had changed since he'd been by years ago home teaching— the blue morning glories in the back, a rose bush come of age.

She shepherded him through the tiny entry of her house and graciously entreated him to sit down on the couch in the parlor. She chose for herself a white cane rocker, much like one he had at home.

Her parlor was a quiet room, gracefully old-fashioned. She had kept it the way she liked it, the way it had always been; she'd explained that to him years ago. She wanted the room always to belong to her and to the ones she had loved. The light that came down through her windows was stained coral as it passed through the ruffled curtains, and it burnished itself warm and glowing against the fine wooden floor. Sitting in that room, he felt something in his mind begin to relax.

She was talking to him, telling him about the people who had left the ward, asking him questions about his mission, but without obliging him to answer.

"And now that you're home?" she asked. It was a question he couldn't have answered, not even politely.

"I wanted to show you something," she went on, almost as though she hadn't asked the question.

She pointed at a low table just to the right of the couch. A number of heavy and vintage leather-bound tomes were stacked there.

"I would like you to look through that top book," she said.

Obediently he leaned over and hefted the thing onto his lap. He looked at her, thinking she might have some explanation she wanted to give him. She waved him on.

He lifted the cover. The cover leaf was inscribed magnificently with her whole name.

"Did you write this?" he asked.

"My husband had a beautiful hand," she said.

He looked at the name for a moment more, and then put the page gently over. On the next page and the subsequent pages were pasted newspaper clippings. They were reviews of piano concerts, of prestigious ones, the clippings from New York papers, and from San Francisco, Philadelphia, Boston, Chicago. He was shocked to realize that this was Sister Krause he was reading about.

The reviews were astoundingly impressive. She had been brilliant. And she'd been beautiful; there were pictures—a lovely young girl with dark hair, wearing charming old-fashioned clothes and laughing into the camera. There were some pictures of her with her husband, both glowingly young.

He turned the pages slowly, and then he looked up at her speechlessly.

"It was a long time ago," she said.

He was deeply ashamed. What this *nice old lady* had been. And what she must be still. He remembered how patronizing he'd been when she'd talked to him about his playing; he colored now with chagrin at the thought of it.

He looked down at the book again, and the eyes of the girl in the pictures held him. He looked back at old Sister Krause, and he found that they were the same eyes. *She's trapped inside of there,* he thought, and then he realized how young and stupid he was.

He looked around the room. "There's no piano here," he said, as anyone else might have said, "You have no walls, or floors, or plumbing."

"Arthritis," she said, holding up her crippled hands. He'd noticed them before, but he hadn't given them more than a distantly sympathetic thought. "I played as long as I could, but in the end I couldn't play anymore. I don't keep a piano now."

His heart twisted inside his chest.

"Oh, it's not that bad," she said. "I know it sounds tragic, but it's really not that bad. I've always had rather a nice gift of music. I hear it in my mind, Sidney, whether anyone's playing it or not. It really doesn't matter if I have a piano; I still have all the music I need right here." She tapped at her temple. "You know, Beethoven did some of his loveliest work when he was quite deaf." She held his eyes now; he couldn't have looked away if he'd wanted to. "I'll tell you what was infinitely worse for me," she said. "It was when I was still very young, and all of that music inside me suddenly seemed to dry up and vanish. *That* was a tragedy. At least at the time I thought it was."

He pulled back as if she had struck him.

"It was a very hard time for me. It's not something you can talk about with other people. They don't understand. Someone who hasn't felt that kind of thing can't know how devastating it can be to lose it."

She had given the thing a name. It was wonderful that she understood, and it was horrible because he had suddenly come up hard against the reality of it. He was frozen there, staring at her, and he was sure that there were tears running down his face.

She nodded. "I think the worst thing," she said thoughtfully, "is feeling that you're alone in all the universe. Claude, my husband, had no music at all. His gift was love. Everyone has his own gift, you know, Sidney." There was a little lamp on the sideboard beside her chair. The lamp was hung with prisms and it spilled dozens of small rainbows on the wall behind the old woman's chair.

She held out something. Carefully putting her book aside, he stirred himself to accept it—a handkerchief, monogrammed *CK* in one corner. He sat down on the couch again, embarrassed, and wiped his face.

"Claude could never understand why I could feel so blue over such a little thing. And, in a way, he was right; I still had *him*, and that really was the most important thing." She smiled at something she was seeing or hearing inside. "He was such a dear man. And I don't believe he ever lost his gift."

She pointed at the table. "Pick up the other book there." Sidney did as he was told. "As you go through it, you may notice that there is a gap of several months. I believe it was from February to May?" She was right. There were no articles pasted in this book that represented those months.

"So, it did come back," he said, terrified that she might tell him it hadn't.

"It did," she said. He sighed. His head ached.

"Every time it happened, eventually, the music did come back."

He looked up at her, horrified. "You mean, this happened more than once?"

She smiled. "It happened a few times," she said. "Not many."

"*Why?*" he asked.

She shrugged, a little birdlike gesture. "I think it must have something to do with stress. If you get too tired, too disoriented —everything these days is stress related." She smiled at him "It's a sort of spiritual thing, isn't it, Sidney? And worldly things can get in the way—worries, troubles. And it can be a horrible spiral; what begins with stress makes you afraid, and that makes more stress, and it makes you more afraid, until you are all tangled up inside. With me—with us—we were childless. And we wanted a little child so badly. I was sure that God was punishing us. I remember," she said sadly, "I began to draw away from everything I loved."

And then she brightened. "But that's a story for another day," she said. "Now, do you want to know what I learned? Because that's why I really wanted you to come up here."

"You knew about me?" he said quietly.

"It takes one," she said, the amusement bright in her old eyes, "to know one. I knew what you were the first moment I heard you play."

He nodded. He, himself, had not been as observant. "Tell me what you learned," he said. "Please."

"I found out that you have to settle yourself," she said, rising. "Stay calm. Stay close to God; it is *his* gift to you, after all. Work on your technique. You can always work on that, and it gives you something constructive to do. Above all, find something or someone outside of yourself and get interested in it. Forget yourself. Everything will be all right. And come back up and see me when you can. Let me know when things are fine again." Her eyes danced. "But you won't have to tell me. I'm sure I'll be able to hear it."

She had escorted him to the door. He found himself out on the tiny porch again, the door closed behind him. He stood there for a moment, wondering why he hadn't thanked her. He was tempted to knock, but understood that that was not the way things wanted to be. So he touched the door lightly with one hand and then left, finding his way homeward under her roses and down her green path.

There was only one thing on Sidney's mind all the way home. "Work on your technique," she'd said. "That's something you can do." And she was right; he was sure his technique needed some work. And it just could be that it would be a little like priming the pump. Something was obviously *stuck* inside of him somewhere, and a little bit of pushing might just make things come loose.

He kicked himself mentally for staying away from the piano for this long. *Who knows?* he told himself. *It might have just*

*taken a couple of hours of noodling around to get things going
again.*

When he got inside the house, he went straight to the music
cabinet and hauled out everything he had. He didn't actually
have a lot of music. Anything remotely rock 'n' roll he'd never
had any need for. He had a couple of hymnals, some classical
collections, and a fat old book of '60s hits. He dropped the little
pile on the floor beside the piano bench and pulled something out
of it—"Bagatelles." He sat down on the bench, opened the key-
board, put his hands in his lap, and took a quiet breath. Then he
put his hands on the keyboard and scanned the music.

It was not very pleasant going. The music didn't make a lot of
sense to him, and his fingers wouldn't do what the music wanted
them to do. He played it slowly first, not because he wanted to.
Then he played it faster, because he didn't care how it sounded,
and then, bored to death by it, he put the book aside.

He picked up some Hanon exercises, feeling that they might
give him a little bit of work. He opened the book to the middle,
and he commenced playing the pattern he'd chosen, beginning
deep in the bass and moving slowly, deliberately up through the
octaves. He worked at it for a long time, and then he chose
another one. But the truth of the matter was that he didn't know
what he was doing. And he wasn't getting the results he'd hoped
to get.

He chose another pattern, and he worked it and he worked it,
up and down the keyboard until he felt as though he'd been hack-
ing at it all his life. He finally slammed his hands down on the
keyboard in disgust and frustration, and was nearly startled to
death when someone behind him yelped in protest.

He turned around and saw his sister sitting on the couch, a
book on her lap and her hand over her heart.

"You scared me to death," she said.

"Same to you," he told her. "When did you come in here?"

"What do you mean, when did I come in? I was sitting here
when *you* came in. I've been sitting here the whole time."

"You were not," he said.

"Sidney," she said, her eyes going all dark and liquid and sad on him, "I asked you where you'd been, and you never even answered me."

He felt a little ashamed. "I had some things on my mind," he said. "Why didn't you ask me again?"

Her eyes went to the piano, then she looked at him again. "I didn't want to disturb you," she said. There was something in her tone; she didn't want to scare him off the piano is what she meant.

"I'm not made of glass," he said. "What are you reading?"

"*Rebecca*," she said, holding up the book. Suddenly he was tired. The room was getting dark. "You hungry?" she asked him.

The thought hadn't occurred to him. "I don't think so," he said. "I think I'm going to go to bed and read something. But you go ahead and eat, okay? And don't worry about me."

She nodded. He shut the piano. "I'm going to go ahead and finish this book tonight," she said. He left the music where it was and went to his room. Just before he shut the door, he heard Courtney saying to herself, "At least there's going to be one good catharsis around here tonight."

Miri had not been expecting company. When she answered the door, expecting to find a salesman standing in the slanting afternoon light on her stoop, there was young Sidney instead. He was leaning back against the porch railings, hands in his pockets, looking very sober and a touch uncomfortable.

"Hello," she said as he straightened up.

"Miri," he said, looking first at her and then at his shoes. She almost smiled. He was so young, and so *intense*. "I've done something," he went on, "without asking you first. I'm hoping you won't mind." He looked up at her with those dark, direct eyes of his. She waited for him to go on, wondering what on earth he could have done that would concern her.

"I bought a piano," he said, inclining his head towards the drive. Out on the street she could see a truck. "It's for you, but it's not for you. That's why I bought it. For me. I want you to teach me." He held up one finger, forestalling her reaction. "I can't do it alone," he said. "I tried." He looked out at the truck. "I know you don't play anymore." He looked at her again. "But you *know*. You know what I don't know. No one's ever *taught* me anything."

She wasn't sure how she felt about it. Distressed, primarily — and moved. "There are better teachers," she said.

He shook his head.

She steadied herself against the door and stood very straight. "I'm not an easy teacher," she told him.

He shook his head again. "You understand me," he said. Now he was pleading.

It was something she hadn't thought of for a long time, something she wasn't sure she had the strength for anymore. He wasn't looking at her now. He had the sense to let her make up her own mind. She studied him in that privacy he had given her, and she saw places under his eyes that looked to her like bruises. It was compassion that decided her—the memory of youth and of her own personal tragedies.

"If you're willing to work," she said.

"I am."

"Every Tuesday night," she told him.

"What time?" he asked.

"Six-thirty. I go to bed early."

"One more question, Miri," he said. He smiled at her, and the bruises all but disappeared. She looked up at him, ready for his question.

"Where do you want the piano?"

Ten

"No. No. No. No. No!" Miri sat back in exasperation.

Sidney dropped his hands on his lap and didn't say anything. He had played maybe half a scale before she stopped him.

"Do it again," she directed, pointing at the keyboard and sitting up, her bright eyes sharp.

He took a respectable breath and put his hands on the instrument again. He played two notes of the sequence.

"Stop," she said. "Keep your hands there. Look at this." She indicated his hands.

"What?" he said.

"You can't expect to play like that," she said.

"I've played like that all my life," he told her.

"Not anymore," she said. She picked up the baton she had been holding in her lap. She held it out and poked it at his hands. He pulled his hands away—a reflex. "Leave them there," she said. "Consider this my own finger." She used the baton to change his hand position, lifting a finger, pushing down a wrist. "Now," she said. "Play it like that."

He looked down at his hands in dismay. "I don't—" he started.

"Play it."

He began to play. "Take it slowly if you have to," she said. He took it very slowly. "No," she said. "This _must_ be kept down."

"Miri . . . ," he said.

"Do you want to learn?" she asked him.

He sighed. "Yes."

"Play it again."

He played it again. She stopped him again, and then again.

"Do you understand what I'm showing you?" she asked.

He looked down at his hands, unhappy.

"Can you remember the position?"

"I believe so," he said.

"Then go home. I can't do any more with you until you can do this. Come back when you can do it."

The lesson had lasted all of twenty minutes.

"All right," he said. He closed the book she had given him.

"Are you sure you want to go through with this?" she asked him. This she asked gently, no longer a teacher, but a friend.

He considered, sighing. "I'll work on my hands," he said. "I'll be back." He stood up. He looked down at her and said, "Do I really have to hold my hands that way?"

"There are classic forms," she said. "What we're doing here is technique. So for these purposes, yes, you have to hold your hands that way."

He nodded, resigned.

"Come back when you can," she said. She looked tired.

He nodded again. "Well, goodnight. I'll let myself out."

She watched him go. She heard the door close behind him, heard him trying the door to make sure it had locked properly. She sat back against the chair and closed her eyes.

"Would you mind," Sidney asked, catching Courtney's arm as she walked by, "if I went with you and Susan tonight?"

"To Miri's?" she asked.

He started playing the piano again. "Yes," he said.

"Aren't you hungry?" she asked. "You know what time it is?"

"What time is it?" He was feeling a little empty, now that she mentioned it.

"It's after three. You've been on that piano since ten o'clock this morning, Sonny. You should be starving." She had her hair in a fat dark braid, and she flipped it over her shoulder. He stopped playing and looked at her. She had a plate of cold pizza. She shook her head at him and started to walk away.

"Wait a second," he said. He looked pointedly at the pizza.

"*Have* it," she said. She put the plate down on the piano. He picked up a piece. "Wait. I'll get you a napkin," she said. He took a bite of it, and he realized how hungry he really was.

She handed him a napkin. He wiped his fingers on his jeans, then took the napkin. "*Sidney*," she said, glaring at him. He looked at her in surprise. She was looking down at his leg. He looked down there, too, wondering what was wrong.

"You wipe your fingers on your pants?" she said indignantly.

"They're dirty," he said, looking down at his pants.

"They are now," she agreed. She sat on the couch and sighed.

And then it struck him that she *was* doing all of his laundry, after all. He thought about that for a moment, and then a vista opened for him temporarily, a vision of his sister cleaning house and cooking and taking care of him, and he—Sidney—being more than a bit of a pain most of the time.

"Does this music drive you crazy?" he asked. "I mean, it's the same thing over and over again all day. It must drive you crazy."

She looked almost frightened. "No," she said. "Don't even think that. I think it's making all of us a little sane." She smiled at him, but it wasn't a very convincing smile.

He had finished the pizza. "Okay, then," he said, using the napkin carefully and turning again to his keyboard, "I've still got a couple of hours to work."

"You got a *piano*," Susan said. She'd spotted it the moment she stepped into the parlor. "It's *beautiful*." She ran her hands over the smooth old mahogany curves.

Sidney put his hand under her elbow and pulled her gently away. "If you will allow me just a few moments here," he said, "I'd like to show Miri something, and then I'll be out of your way."

"Sit down for a moment," Miri said, almost apologetically, patting Susan's arm and sending her over to the couch. Courtney followed. Susan looked at Courtney, and Courtney shrugged. They sat.

Sidney had placed a chair by the piano, and, having helped Miri into it, settled himself on the piano bench. He put his hands on the keyboard and seemed to take a long breath. Then he began to play. He played what he had been playing all day—the exercises, the exercises. The playing was slow and methodical, but anyone could have felt the fierce determination in it. Susan looked at Courtney once more, but Courtney couldn't explain anything.

He stopped playing and sat there with his hands in his lap.

Miri began to nod. "It's not bad," she said. "Put your hands up again."

He did as she said. She slid the baton off the music stand and tapped his hands, making minute changes here and there in his position. Courtney looked at Susan. Susan nodded, finally satisfied. Courtney sat back into the couch, frowning.

"Do it again," Miri directed.

He went through it all again, and again he played fiercely, as though it were really music he was making. When he had finished, Miri sat back in her chair, regarding him. "You've been working," she observed.

"Yes, ma'am," he said without looking at her.

She sighed. "All right, let's see what you can do with the Bach." She added, "It won't be right."

"I know," he said. He stood up and helped Miri out of her chair, and then he left. A few moments later they heard his car backing out of the drive.

"You're teaching him," Susan said. "How long has this been going on?"

"Since yesterday," Miri said. "He bought the piano." She led the way into the kitchen. Courtney followed, her face troubled.

"You never said you were a musician," Susan said. "Don't you play anymore?"

Miri held up her crippled hands, and Susan colored up.

"I'm sorry. I forgot," she said and then lapsed into silence.

"I didn't know about this," Courtney said. Her voice had a rusty sound to it, as though she hadn't used it for a long time.

Miri looked at her.

"He— " Courtney began, and then she shrugged again and sat down at the old oak table. It was a big kitchen for such a small house, with its large oaken table, too big a room for silence.

"I think I understand," Miri said. "It must not be easy to live with him when he's this way."

"What *way?*" Courtney cried. "That's what I don't *under-stand.* I've never seen him this way before. He doesn't talk to me. He forgets to eat. He isn't aware of anything that goes on around him. I *know* something's wrong. But he won't *talk* to me." She was embarrassed to be crying like this. But it was unbearable that someone in the world should understand her brother and that she could not. Susan came and put her arms around Courtney.

"He's such a brat," Susan said.

"No, he's not," Courtney said. "He's hurting." She put her head down on Susan's shoulder.

Miri smiled at them sadly. "You have to remember, dear," Miri said gently, "your brother is, for good or otherwise, a very gifted person. And he's very young. I know he loves you. Right now, he's just very frightened and selfish."

"Frightened of *what?*" Courtney asked.

Miri shook her head and smiled. "Frightened of not having something he had always taken for granted," she said.

"So, it's not something serious," Susan said.

Miri considered. "Not yet," she said. "But it might be a very good thing for you to get him to talk about it, Courtney. He should understand that he's hurting you. Maybe that would bring him out of it. You might try. Susan, why don't you get out the ice cream? Don't worry, dear heart," she said, her voice at once comforting Courtney and closing the discussion.

"So, how long did you teach?" Susan asked, opening the freezer. She found a box of Kleenex on top of the refrigerator, pulled out a few, and handed them to Courtney.

"Nearly thirty years," Miri said. "I had some very fine students," she said, and then she mentioned a few names that meant nothing at all to Courtney, but seemed to impress Susan very much. "I think your brother could have been one of the best of them, if he'd chosen to be a concert pianist. My gifts weren't like his. I loved to play the music of others. He's one of the ones who make music out of life."

She smiled at Courtney again. "Things will be better soon," she said. "You just practice your own gifts and be patient."

There were few things that frightened Courtney. Personal confrontation was one of them—not because she was afraid to speak, but because she was afraid of making someone else unhappy. The thought of forcing an issue upset her. And she was upset now, sitting on her bed in her robe in the dark, feeling that Miri must be right, that it was time Sidney should talk to somebody, but all the time hoping he would go to bed before she had worked up her courage.

That he didn't want to talk was obvious. It wasn't a question of his love for her; she knew that well enough. It was just that he felt that whatever was bothering him was his own private business. She respected privacy. She was reluctant to violate it.

But Sidney hadn't gone to bed yet; he was still somewhere in the dark, silent house, and it was time for her to find him. She stood up, pulling the robe's belt tighter, her heart beating in her ears. She padded across the floor, opened her door, and went quietly, slowly into the front room.

Sidney was standing in front of the windows, looking out at the sea. She could see him, a dark silhouette against the dim sea and stars, as though he were wrapped up in the deepest part of night. She stopped behind the piano and stood there for some time. It felt strange to her, watching him there, that he should be her brother. She didn't really know him anymore.

She said his name. The rustiness was still there in her voice. She had to say it twice before he turned. He said, "You should be asleep."

"I know," she said. And then they stood there. Of course, it was obvious to him that she had something to say, so he waited. But she didn't know how to start it.

"You're my brother," she said finally. "I love you very much."

"I know that," he told her quietly.

"You've always been my best friend." She leaned against the piano. "Do you know . . ." She blinked hard, trying to keep the tears out of her voice. It was no good. "There's something wrong, here. And . . . ," she shrugged, "I wish you'd talk to me about it."

He hadn't moved. And now, he didn't speak. She was embarrassed because she couldn't stop making all the soft little sounds that come with crying. She hadn't wanted to manipulate him.

"I told you," he said softly. "It's just something . . . I just . . . I wouldn't know how to explain it."

"You could try," she said. "It wouldn't be as hard for me, if I knew what was going on."

He was quiet. Then he said sadly, "Has it been so hard?"

And it hadn't. Not really. She loved the house, and she loved Susan and Calvin and Miri and her place with them. But with Sidney, yes, it had been hard, because the thing that could have been happening between them had been so pitifully undeveloped.

"I love you," she said again. "And there's something hurting you."

She heard him sigh. "Why don't you sit down?" he said. She came out from behind the piano. She saw him point towards the couch. He sat down in the white cane chair. He put his feet up on the little glass table and rested his head on the back of the chair.

"A long time ago," he said, still softly, as if the dark needed gentle handling, "I tried to tell you about . . ." he sighed again . . . "the way I hear things, about the music I have inside of me. You remember?"

"Yes," she said, desperately hauling out the dim memory.

"Well, it's not there anymore."

And that was all. She waited for the rest of it, but that was all. She had fortunate instincts, and she said nothing for a moment, trying to make herself understand the significance of what he had said.

"You can still play," she said.

He was quiet. He shifted in the chair. "I think I know how it is for you when you read," he said. "I think, when you read, the images are real for you. Like, you're really *there.* Isn't that how it is?"

"Yes," she said. It was more than that for her, really, but the words were fairly approximate.

"It's different for me. I feel things. And I hear the words. But I'm never really *there.* You know, I don't even read the descriptions."

"Sidney," she said.

"I hate 'em," he said, and there was some laughter in his voice.

"They're the best part," she told him.

"What if one day," he settled himself and folded his hands across his chest, "you opened a book, and you couldn't read anymore. What if you looked at the words, and they didn't mean anything. You had to sound them out, each one of them, letter by letter. It wouldn't be the same, would it?"

"No," she said.

"And all the feeling in the words would escape you, because all you could see were the units of sound. And because of that, you couldn't even speak. What if you were full of anger, or love, or any kind of feeling, and you couldn't speak or sing or express it? You think you could just go on and live your life? You think you could just go on and make life pleasant for everybody? Wouldn't it make you afraid of what else you could lose?"

She didn't understand. No, she *did*—she understood the words he was saying, and she could imagine what they meant, but she couldn't *be* him.

"Miri says it will all come back," he said, but it was what Miri believed, and not what he believed. "Sooner or later. I'm not sure what I'm supposed to do in the meantime—sell shoes, maybe." He spoke not so much with bitterness as with despair.

"There are people who sell shoes," she said, stung.

"It's not what I do," he said. And she was sorry she had taken offense.

"You're not worried about the money," she said. He couldn't have been. He already had more of it than he would ever need.

"I'm worried," he said—angry now, or frustrated or impatient— "about *me*. There's nothing of *me* left. There's this man who walks around looking like me, but there's nothing inside of him—"

"It's not true," she said.

"It's *true*. And I told you I didn't want to talk about it. You can't understand this unless it happens to you." He stood up and went to the windows again. She knew he was angry because he thought she wasn't trying to understand him.

"So," she said, "whatever's left of you, you throw that in the garbage, right? You don't salvage anything." He didn't answer.

"There's plenty left inside of you, Sidney," she said, "only, that's where you're keeping it. You're making up a situation here.

It doesn't have to be that way." This wasn't helping. She didn't want to alienate him, and that's just what she was doing. "I say this because I love you. I *love* you. I don't want you digging yourself into a hole. If Miri says it'll come back, it'll come back. You believe in God. Tell him you need it back. Sidney, I'm sorry." And now she was crying again. "I want you to be happy."

He laughed. "You sound like mother," he said, not unkindly.

"Thanks a lot," she said. But it had made her feel better immediately, that he should joke.

"Why did you lose it?" she asked. The question took all the laughter out of him.

"Miri says it's probably stress," he said flatly.

"You're not doing much to unstress yourself," she said.

"I'm trying."

"Don't *try*."

He laughed again, but it wasn't a happy sound. "I'll try not to."

"I really am on your side," she said.

"And you really do sound like mother," he said.

"Maybe she was right," Courtney said.

"I don't know." He turned his back to her and looked out at the ocean. "Thanks for the love."

There was nothing more to say. At least she knew what she was up against. "Don't kill yourself," she said suddenly, almost before she'd thought it.

"I may be a little crazy right now," he said, turning away from the window, "but, my dear, dear sister, I'm not *stupid*."

She closed her eyes. *We'll get through this,* she told herself. And she felt better.

"I'll be here," she said.

"I know," he said. She could hear the smile in it.

She waited another moment, and then she said, "Good night." She stood up. And then he spoke again, but so softly, she wasn't sure at first whether he was talking to her.

"You're my best friend, Courtney," he said. "You've always been my best friend." He turned slightly, not enough so that he could look at her. "I don't want you to think I don't know what's going on here. It must be hard to live with somebody who's from a different planet than you are most of the time. This isn't the way I wanted it. Sometimes I feel like I'm trapped inside of myself and I can't get out." He was still almost whispering. "I've never been so scared."

"You've lost things before," she said gently.

"Not like this," he said. "Not without some kind of touch-stone."

She felt his isolation as if it were an aura of cold about him, and she knew he had generated it for himself. "You have me," she said, trying not to let any of her mother's reproach into her voice, "and Susan and Calvin and Miri and everyone else. And you have God. Love is a touchstone, Sidney. It may be the only one."

He had turned back to the window. She didn't know whether he had heard her. She was disappointed in the words; they sounded empty and didactic. The fact was that she had tried to give him something of herself; the thing was true for her. The love she had for her people had been the only thing she could tie to. "Good night," she said again, and she put her hand out to touch the piano as she found her way around it.

In the hallway she paused and looked back. He was standing in front of the window again, singular and dark, the night pulled in once more securely around him.

Eleven

"It isn't Tuesday again," Miri said, as if she, herself, were a bit unsure. She was standing in the doorway of her house, facing the increasingly ubiquitous young male caller who was standing there on her porch, music under his arm, hands buried in the pockets of his jacket.

"No, ma'am," he said to her. "It's Thursday afternoon."

"You can't keep up like this, you know," she told him. "I'm too old for it."

"I spent the whole morning on it and the afternoon up till just now." He held out the Bach. "I can't do any more till I know what I'm supposed to be doing."

"You're pushing it too hard," she said.

"Three months from now, I have to be in good enough shape to do an album. Any _minute_ now, the word's going to be out that I'm back and some contractor is going to call me, expecting me to play some gig for somebody in the studio. When that happens, if I can't perform, it'll be the last call I get. I don't think I'm pushing myself too hard. But maybe I'm pushing you too hard."

She met his eyes and saw the terrible determination-born-of-panic in them. She stood back against the door and waved him on inside.

He was already sitting on the piano bench when she entered the room, her chair waiting beside him. He was spreading his music as she came up behind him. He stood and helped her into her seat. She leaned over and slid the baton out from behind the stand and held it in her lap.

She closed her eyes for a moment. When she opened them, she said, "You may begin."

He played three bars before she stopped him. "Here," she said, using the baton to point out the places in the music. "Here and here. Precision. This was written for a harpsichord. We want no dynamics. Keep this wrist *down*."

He started to play again, his face hard with concentration. She allowed him a bar or two more than the last time, and then she stopped him again.

"It was precise," he said, his voice edged with frustration.

"A jackhammer is also precise. You mustn't think that because there are no dynamics there should be no sensitivity. Play it again. Wait. Take a moment to set yourself. Play."

He took a long breath, closing his eyes as he did. He opened his eyes, set his face, and started once more.

Once more she stopped him.

He brought his hands up off the keyboard and made fists out of them. He muttered angrily and came up off the bench. He shoved his hands into his pockets and made his way over to the windows. He turned away from the windows, pacing the length of the room and then back. He took his hands out of the pockets and pulled at his hair with them.

"This used to be so *easy*," he hissed. He took a few more turns up and down the room then sat down on the bench again, his frustration not at all vented.

"Did that help?" she asked.

"No."

"Go home," she said. "You are too angry. You'll never learn anything good with anger inside you like this. I can't teach this anger."

"I'm not angry," he said with an evenness that attested to great self-control.

"Don't lie to me," she said, her passion equal to his own. "But more important, don't lie to yourself. You *are* angry. Because you're afraid. And as long as you are angry, and as long as you're afraid, you will not get what you want. Because an angry man cannot *listen*."

"I'm listening," he said.

"You are *not*," she said.

He sat silent for a time, his cheeks a high red and his breathing hard. He rubbed his nose with the back of one hand. "Okay," he said. "What am I not hearing?"

"The music," she said.

He turned to her, his eyes full of pain.

"You misunderstand me," she said. "There is more to hear than the thing you have lost. There is an understanding that comes through your eyes, through the rhythms of your own self, your blood, the hours of your days, through love. You are treating the music as if it were a *thing* and an enemy." She touched his wrist with the end of the baton. "You are thinking that the whole world is your enemy."

He remained silent, staring at the music. "You feel like the world is a cage, and that God is your enemy," she said.

"No," he said.

"What then?" she asked, putting the baton back into her lap.

"There is a reason for this," he said slowly.

"What reason?" she asked.

"There has to be a reason," he said.

"Why?"

He folded his arms. Then he unfolded them and scratched at a tiny spot on the knee of his jeans.

"So, you're telling me that there is a reason why God *did* this to you?" she said.

He looked at her. "Yes."

"But you aren't angry with God," she said.

"No." He was looking at the music again.

"Why not?" she asked. "If someone did such a thing to me, I would be angry, too."

"I'm not *angry*," he reminded her. "*You* said I was angry."

"Why aren't you angry?" she asked again.

"Because, the Lord . . ." He looked at his hands. "Somehow, this is . . ."

"You deserved this," she said. "It's a punishment."

"No," he said, but he said it as if the idea were not foreign to him. "Perhaps I needed this."

"You needed this," she repeated. "Why?"

"I don't know," he said, misery close to the surface. "Pride. I don't know. There's a reason."

"He's punishing you for your pride," she said.

"No," he said. But he wasn't sure—not really.

"He's punishing you because you loved it too much," she went on, "because your priorities weren't right."

"Maybe he's just trying to *teach* me that my priorities aren't straight," he said.

"By making you miserable," she finished.

" 'I give unto men weakness . . .' " he said.

"Now *there*," she said, shaking the baton at him, "*there* you may have a point. The Lord gives a man weaknesses—he gave you your hands. He gave you your body. He gave you your chemistry, your passion—now you see what you have done with these weaknesses. You are succumbing to them. You let your unhappiness stand in the way of your reason, your knowledge."

"There's more to it than that," he said.

"So the Lord visited this . . ."—she held up her crippled hands—"on me? It was to teach me about priorities? I had pride. I loved the music. So he took it away from me to teach me that there is more in life? This is a gift of God?"

He looked away, unable to answer.

"You aren't thinking. And tell me this—what is the rest of the scripture? Has this ordeal you are going through—has it made you humble? What have you done to turn this weakness— How have you used it to make strength? What are you learning? Have you, in your humility, turned to God for help? Or have you held yourself away from him?" She poked him with the baton once more. "You forget. I went through this, too."

She sat back. She was tired, but when he looked at her, he saw that her eyes were very bright.

"As for the other thing," she went on. "I don't think you're right."

"What other thing?" he asked.

"When you said that it was easier for you before. *This* that we are doing now—it would have been no easier for you before. Maybe it would have been harder. Your technique is awful. You've gotten away with it in the past because of your gift. You will be better for this when you get it back. But the technique will still be hard, even then. Perhaps more so."

He sighed.

She used the baton to close the music. "Go home," she told him. "Think about what I've said. I've told you what I believe. And I can *not* teach you until you understand it. Don't even touch the piano until you understand it. You came to me. This is what I am telling you."

He picked up the music.

"Leave it here," she directed. "Go home."

He stood up, awkwardly. She smiled at him, but he didn't see it. He turned to go, stopped himself, came back to help her up. Then he left without another word. She was not surprised. She shook her head, smiling, as the door closed behind her, and then stood in the middle of the room, trying to remember what it was she had been doing before he came. Whatever it had been, she could now go about it with more energy.

_____ *Twelve*

"He always wins when we play singles like this," Calvin mused, looking ruefully down at the Trivial Pursuit board. One of the little round trays had all its tokens tucked neatly away inside. The rest of the trays were not as fortunate. "It must be because he didn't go to college."

"Will you get in here and finish this *game*?" Susan called. Sidney was off doing something in the kitchen while everyone else waited for him to take his turn. "Though why I should say that, I don't know. You could at least be graceful about winning," she told him as he came in, a small carton of french yogurt in his hand. "Keeping a low profile would help. Next time, we play teams. The three of us against you."

In the end Calvin won. Sidney's luck and his willingness to fish in the back of his brain for stray facts had both worn thin. It was the usual Thursday soiree, with pie all around, and some good, lazy conversation. Calvin beguiled the women with talk of court, and Sidney ate his yogurt in silence.

"Someone started to paint my beach fence about a week ago," Susan said. "But suddenly . . . ," she parted her hands, giving them to understand that the painter had just vanished.

"I'll finish it," Sidney said with exaggerated patience.

"He's on drugs," Calvin said serenely.

"He is not," Courtney said, not finding the comment terribly funny.

"He's a musician," Calvin pointed out.

"Leave me alone," Sidney told him.

"I'm going to do the dishes," Susan said. Courtney immediately got up and started gathering the plates and forks.

"I've got to go," Calvin said. "I have to be in the office early tomorrow."

Sidney looked up. "I'll walk you out," he said. Calvin pulled on his jacket and opened the front door. The air was brisk, and there was the usual breeze from off the sea. Sidney followed Calvin out to the drive and around to the leeward side of the car. Calvin opened his door, and Sidney watched him silently. Calvin closed the door again and leaned against it.

"All right, what?" he asked.

Sidney shivered a little because of the wind. He shifted his weight. "You were telling me once," he said, "about people adjusting to being home." He squinted at Calvin, and he folded his arms, hugging himself to keep the chill off.

Calvin hunkered down beside the car, keeping the wind off. "Get out of the wind," he said. Sidney crouched down near the rear bumper. "Okay," Calvin said, "So?"

"So. What's the adjustment? I mean . . ." He looked over at the house. He could see one of the kitchen lights glowing amber in the dark. It looked warm. "Something's not right," he said. "My stomach's in knots."

Calvin looked down at his hands. "I can tell you how I see things," he offered. "Not that it's necessarily the truth."

"Okay," Sidney said.

"I don't know. It seems . . . ," Calvin said, going carefully, "you spend two years doing one particular, peculiar kind of work. And it's a discipline. Depending on your mission president, a fairly strict discipline. Everything, right? When you get up, where you go, what you do. Some of it's because to do the work, you have to have the right spirit and the knowledge. Some of it's because you're young and still a jerk, and you wouldn't do it right if there weren't a rule about it.

"And then you get home. And you think, 'Man, I'm *home*,' and inside you want to make it like it used to be. But the thing is, in those two years, you've changed. You're older for one thing. And for another thing, you've been on this sort of rich spiritual diet. And you forget all that because you're home. But it doesn't work that way. You still need the spiritual diet. Okay, your function may be different now, but your purpose is still the same. Your orientation should still be the same. So you go back to the old things, and they don't look the same anymore. You drop the new things, and you go hungry. You don't just have this working relationship with God one minute, and then drop completely out of it the next and expect to feel great, you know what I mean?"

Sidney nodded slowly, still chilling.

"So you have to learn to mix the two things. In the world, but not of the world, more or less. You have to fix yourself on a new function and go with it, but you have to go with it the new way. That's all. And love everybody. And be perfect. And I'm freezing to death out here. So, is that what you wanted?"

Sidney nodded again.

"Good," Calvin said. He got up and opened the door and folded himself into the seat. "Let's finish Susan's fence Saturday," he said.

Sidney nodded, dancing a little to stir up some warmth.

The door of his house opened, and he saw Susan come out. She waved and went off towards her house. "Nice girl," Calvin said.

Sidney nodded again. "So's your sister," Calvin said. He pulled the door closed and started the car. Sidney stood there for a minute. When Calvin started to back out, Sidney went back to the house.

It was a pure sensual joy, walking back into that warm little house. He wandered into the kitchen, looking for Courtney, and found her seated at the table with a pen in her hand and paper before her.

"Where've you been?" she asked. "Your cute little cheeks are all red."

He put a pan of water on the stove to boil. "Talking to Calvin," he said. "What're you doing?"

"Writing to Mother," she said, giving him a strange, but not unpleasant, look.

A slow, creeping horror came on him as he looked at the pen in her hand, "You know, I haven't written to her yet," he said, "I keep forgetting. She's going to kill me. I *forgot*. She's going to think I forgot."

"Undoubtedly," Courtney said. She frowned down at the paper. "It's so hard to write to her. No matter what I tell her, next time she writes, she's going to drop those little *hints* that I haven't done something I ought to have done, or that something I did wasn't quite the right thing—always some gentle, little wounded hint. I hate getting those letters."

He sat down at the table. "That doesn't sound like you," he said.

"Well, you know what I mean?" she asked. "She's always so worried that everybody do their *duty* by her. What I want is to have my mother for a friend. And all she wants is for me to do everything she thinks I *ought* to do. It's not easy to write these letters. I can't talk to her for three minutes without getting jumped on. She reads meanings into everything I say—and never good meanings. I guess it's easier to write. Sidney," she said, looking at him, "I don't like Mother. And I *hate* feeling that way."

"You love her," Sidney said.

"Yes. But I don't like her."

He nodded. "I don't think she likes herself," he said.

"I know," Courtney said, looking down at the paper unhappily.

"Come on, old girl," he said. He was feeling unaccountably better. "We'll write it together. And we'll give our dear mama something to think about anyway, eh?"

"You're out of your mind," she said, grinning.

"And it's a good thing," he said, taking the paper away from her.

"Would you mind telling me," Courtney said, leaning back against the kitchen cabinets and shoving the sleeves of her sweatshirt up above her elbows, "*why* my brother, Sidney, hasn't eaten anything for the last two days?"

Calvin, smelling of turpentine and paint and the wild sea air, had come down the beach to Courtney's kitchen, ostensibly for a drink of water. Now he stood, wiping his hands on a filthy rag, his face a study of misgiving. "Nothing?"

"Nothing."

Calvin nodded. The very thought of it made him feel dismal. "It sure smells nice in here," he said.

"What you smell in here, my friend," Courtney said, indicating the stove with her flat of her hand, "is temptation, pure and simple. Honestly, I'm beginning to think he really is irrational. Last night I made fried chicken. It was beautiful. And you know what he did?"

Calvin's unhappy look deepened. "What?" he asked.

"He looked at me with this very noble, very *deep* look, and he went out and took a walk."

"So, you do have some of it left over," Calvin said with a sigh.

"So, judging by the look and the air of sacrifice, I assumed it was some sort of religious gesture. Could this be true?"

"Fasting," Calvin said. "You couldn't have eaten it all by yourself. Perhaps Susan came over—"

"Calvin. There *is* chicken in the refrigerator; it is *Sidney* we are discussing here, if you don't mind."

"Obviously, he's fasting," Calvin said, his eyes wandering over to the refrigerator.

"Obviously. But where I come from the only people who fast are either in the Bible and dead now, which is understandable, or they are saints and dead now, which is also understandable. And Sidney will also be dead if he doesn't eat something. And he is not a saint. And I thought you people only fasted on the first Sunday of every month. And then just for breakfast."

Calvin's face took on a patience that was itself nearly holy. "My dear girl," he said, "how many weeks have you been among us, not to know such a thing. We people fast whenever the mood comes on us—as in whenever we are troubled . . ." He opened the refrigerator door. "Or when we need a miracle, or when we want something very badly. And there are other times . . ." Courtney gently but pointedly moved between Calvin and the refrigerator, forcing the door closed, and—arms folded—placing her person against it. ". . . When we wish to clear our souls for example, or when we seek understanding. Which is something you might like to go for yourself, sometime . . ."

Courtney sighed. "And I have stuffed lamb chops," she lamented.

"I," Calvin reminded her, "am not fasting. Nor is Susan, as far as I can tell. I'm sure that we could prevail on her . . ."

She held up her hand. "I'm sure I wasn't going to invite you anyway," she said. "What am I supposed to do with Sidney?"

"He'll eat. By tomorrow. If he doesn't, I'll talk to him. But he will."

"And what is he going to do this afternoon while the rest of us are eating?" she asked. "Just stay out there and finish that fence himself?"

Calvin nodded. "The very best thing for him."

"What?" Sidney groaned sleepily into his pillow. Nobody should have somebody wake him up early on Sunday morning. Not ever. Not for anything. He turned over and glared at the tousled and sleepy-looking head of his sister, who was peeking around the edge of his bedroom door.

"I'm just trying to decide . . . ," she yawned, "whether to put in a roast before we go, or maybe we should just have soup."

"Soup, if you're tired," he said. Then he added, "Go back to bed," and pulled the covers up over his ears.

"If you're going to eat, I'd rather do the roast," she told him.

He pulled the covers down and squinted at her. "Why wouldn't I eat?" he asked.

She stood there looking at him, her eyes just a touch dull. "Forget I asked," she said. And she shut the door.

Miri had few secrets from herself these days. She knew she was tired, and it didn't frighten her at all. She was more than ready for the other side—to be young again, to be with Claude. But there were still earthly pleasures that held her: this day for instance—a fine balmy spring day just made for garden weeding. She had on a sun hat with wide satin ribbons that tied under her chin, and a cheerful yellow dress and gardening gloves, the small things that were part of the fabric of living.

And there was her family, which needed her now as it never had before, and the children. The children needed her, too,—young Sidney, and Susan—the ones whose souls were crowded and confused. She smiled when she thought of Courtney, because Courtney was so very clear.

She may have exiled him, but Miri had no doubts that Sidney would be up here again, very soon, ready or not. His drive and his desire exhausted her, but the quiet eyes and the strong hands spoke so clearly of the treasures within. He never talked about

himself, but Miri thought there was much she understood any-
way.

And, of course, what she had not known intuitively, Susan
had told her—all about the ravages of Emily on his soul, and
about how honorable he was. Courtney had told Miri a few
things, too, about her own young life. They had done very well
for themselves, the brother and the sister, all things considered.

Now, after a morning's good gardening, Miri was sitting on
her tiny porch, enjoying a neat lunch of lemonade and cheese and
apple slices, with the ocean below and the gulls above for com-
pany. She had been lost in the pleasure of the moment, remem-
bering other such times, when Sidney came.

He stood quietly, outside her private space, waiting. She
became aware of him gradually. And then she turned to him and
smiled patiently. He came forward and stood by the edge of the
porch, a still respectful distance away. He placed a piece of music
manuscript on her lap.

"What's this?" she asked.

"I didn't play," he said quickly. She smiled to herself. "I told
you about the album. The record. I have to do the arrangements.
My friend, C.J.—he's the guitar player in the band—and I, we
got together last night and we worked on this. It's not very
good," he said, "but it's better than I expected."

She nodded. "I don't understand this kind of music much,
myself," she said. It was another language, one that she hadn't
had the energy to learn.

He took the paper out of her lap and looked it over again,
mutely, then he put it aside and pressed his hands together
between his knees. "I can't tell you," he said quietly, "that I really
feel any different than I did three days ago. But I'm trying. I
really am trying." He paused. "I'm hoping the effort will be
enough for you."

She sighed. He looked up at her. She looked down into those
eyes and found them depthless, as she found almost all eyes these
days. He *was* trying. She had to give him what she could while
she still could.

"We can try, Sidney," she said. "That's all we can ever do."
She sighed again and looked out into the sky. *It's strange,* she

thought, *to live where you can look straight out across your backyard into the sky.* "And I suppose you want to start again right now."

"If that's all right," he said, the excitement transparent in his voice.

She nodded, looking at him. There was still that tightness to his jaw. He got up. "You go on in," she said. "I'll finish my apples." He brushed off his jeans and picked up his poor manuscript and took all the stairs in one stride.

He's still grim, and he's still tense, she thought as he disappeared through her front door, *but something has changed. He seemed a little happier, a little less angry, certainly excited. Well,* she thought to herself, *I think we might finally be able to get somewhere.*

Thirteen

"It's for you," someone was saying. Emily had been trying futilely all night to take a simple standard deviation for her statistics class. She'd gone over it a hundred times, the same numbers, the same sampling.

"_Emily,_" the voice hissed, and someone was poking her shoulder. "The _phone_ is for you."

Emily opened her eyes into the dark. "What?" she asked.

"The _phone._ The _phone._ Next time it's for you and it's two-thirty in the morning, you can just get up and answer it _yourself._" The voice receded, mumbling, and Emily was left by herself in the darkness.

The phone was for her. She pulled herself upright and put her feet out of the bed onto the cold floor. Who calls at two-thirty in the morning? Her mind was still trying to manipulate the statistical material, and now she had the terrors; jerked out of deep sleep that way, she always got the terrors, the shaky hands, the heart pounding, the blood beating in her ears.

The only reason why people call other people at two-thirty in the morning is that something has happened. It might be something very bad, or it might be something very good. As Emily made her way down the hall and into the kitchen, she was thinking it had better—please—be something wonderful.

She shivered and picked up the phone. "Hello?" she said and her stomach clenched.

"Emily?" It was Kinsey. It wasn't going to be something good.

"What's wrong?" Emily asked.

Kinsey hesitated; it was going to be something very bad. Emily huddled in the chair, chilling.

"There's been an accident, Em," Kinsey said.

"Is it Mother?" Emily asked. Strange how the fear was always right there.

"No. The family's fine. Honey, it's Sidney."

"Is he dead?" There it was again, the fear speaking right out loud. She hadn't even heard the question in her own mind before it had been spoken.

"No. But it's bad. Well, it's not that bad. They thought he was critical when they first took him in, but he's stable now."

"What *happened*?" Emily asked, pulling her feet up under her robe. The kitchen floor was icy.

Kinsey sighed. "C.J. was over there working on some music, and they decided to take it over to Graham's to show him what they'd done. C.J. took his own car because we're closer to Graham's than we are to Sidney's. They got out on Route 1 and some drunk kid in a van crossed the lane and plowed right into Sidney. It totalled the car. C.J. said there wasn't anything left but the metal."

"The car . . . ," Emily murmured.

"C.J. said he took one look at the car and knew Sidney was dead. But he got over there and pulled him out. There wasn't anybody on the road; it was so late. Somebody came along with a CB and called an ambulance. C.J. didn't want to move him, but there was gas leaking out everywhere, so he pulled him clear and gave him a blessing."

"So, he's in the hospital."

"C.J. rode in with him. He's stable now."

"I'm coming down," Emily said, standing up.

"No, you're not."

"What if he dies?"

"He's not going to die. And you're not coming down. You're right at the end of your finals. You get in the car and drive down here tonight, and you'll kill yourself. It's foolishness. You're going to be down here in another three days anyway. And anyway, he's not going to die. He got a bad hit on the side of the head, and he's a little cut up, that's all. He had his seat belt on. I shouldn't have called you, but I thought you'd want to know. C.J. just got home."

"I can't leave him down there, Kinsey," Emily said miserably.

There was a little silence on the other end of the phone. "Emily," Kinsey said, insufferably older and wiser, "for one thing, his sister is down here. He's not going to be alone. I've met her. You couldn't do anything for him that she couldn't do. And for another thing, I don't think he's going to want to see you."

Emily sat down in the chair again. "Why not?" she asked, half angry, half afraid.

"Why do you think?" Kinsey was impatient. "Sid told C.J. he'd called you a couple of times in the last few months, and you never returned his calls. I know you write to him. I mean, I assume you still do . . ."

"He's home now," Emily said, meaning he didn't need letters now. "I know if I call him, he'll just put pressure on me, and I can't handle any more pressure right now. This is my last semester. I just had to get this done, and then I could come down there and work at the studio and everything would be done. Until then, I just couldn't afford a relationship."

"What makes you think there's going to be one here waiting for you? I'm telling you, kid, if he wasn't that important to you before, do you think he's going to want you to show up at the hospital now? He's a fairly smart boy, Em. He's going to be able to tell affection from melodrama."

"And what is that supposed to mean?" Emily said, wholly angry now.

"You think about it," her sister said. "I'll tell him you wanted to come. I'll tell him I wouldn't let you. You're going to be down here next week anyway. Call him then. I've got to go. C.J. hasn't had anything to eat."

There was a pause.

"He *is* important to me," Emily said.

"We'll see," Kinsey said.

Emily dropped the phone into its cradle and stood in the middle of the room, listening to the hum of the refrigerator. She took a deep breath, let it out slowly, and made her way back to bed. *You have to do what you have to do,* she told herself. She said it in her mind a hundred times before she fell asleep.

Fourteen

"I don't like the way he looks," Courtney said. She was standing by one of the front windows, watching Sidney walk up and down on the beach outside. Calvin came up and stood beside her. He lifted the edge of the blind and peered out from under it.

"Why's he out there?" Calvin asked. "Seems like he should be in bed."

"Seems like it," Courtney agreed. "But Sidney doesn't listen to anybody but Sidney these days. He won't stay in, because he knows if he stays in, I'm going to be able to see that something's wrong, and I'm going to make him go back to the hospital." She left the window and dropped onto the couch.

"You're angry," Calvin observed. He sat down in Sidney's chair.

"Calvin, I'm _frustrated._ He shouldn't even be home. He bullied everyone at the hospital until they had to let him go. He kept threatening to call _you._"

"Me?" Calvin said. "Why?"

"You're his lawyer."

"That's right," Calvin said. "Sorry."

Courtney slapped her knees and stood up again.

"That bruise looks so _bad._ I mean, it's nearly the whole side of his face. And I know that doesn't have to mean anything. But I _know_ he's in pain. Those sunglasses he's got on out there? The light hurts his eyes. He was wearing them in _here_ this morning. He walks as if he's got a terrific hangover. But he will not—_will not_—even let me _speak_ to him about it. He lies to me. He says he's fine. He's _not_ fine."

"Why should he lie?" Calvin asked, watching her move around the room.

She sat down on the couch again. She had her hair pulled back into a pony tail, and he liked to look at the clean lines of her face. "Because he's scared of hospitals."

"So am I," Calvin said.

"Probably not like he is," she said. "He had his appendix out when he was about twelve. He wouldn't talk about it afterwards. I mean, I know, Sidney is quiet. But when he's upset, it's more than quiet. It's like he draws inward, and he doesn't even want you to make him think about it. He's always been that way. The only thing I really remember is that they put an IV in his hand, and he couldn't play very well for weeks afterwards because his hand hurt him. Fortunately, this time Dr. Moody was at the hospital by the time Sidney got there, and he took care of things. He's just terrified of the hospital."

"Have you talked to the doctor?" Calvin asked.

"Yes," Courtney said, huddling miserably into the corner of the couch. "What can he do? You can't argue with Sidney. He'll just tell Dr. Moody to find himself another patient. Stubborn idiot."

The tears in the girl's eyes were terribly compelling. "I could talk to him," Calvin offered. He would have offered anyway, but the tears made it so much more pleasant.

"Thank you," she said. She smiled at Calvin. And then she shrugged. "It wouldn't do any good. Why don't you wait? Sooner or later, somebody's going to have to do something. It's just a matter of waiting until the right time. I just hope we don't time it wrong."

Sidney had wedged himself into a nice, cozy corner in the little studio Graham kept above his garage. He stood there with his arms folded, watching Graham at the piano. Graham was playing at the chart C.J. and Sidney had done together.

Sidney could see Graham's wife and kids fooling around in the back yard, down below. The kids were in the pool. Nancy, in a bathing suit with a shirt thrown over it, was weeding a flower bed. Sidney was noticing that Nancy looked pretty good for a woman who'd hit forty. And then he thought that Graham's eighteen-year-old daughter was looking pretty good these days, too.

Sidney pulled his eyes away from the window and flicked them across Graham's back. Then he fixed them on the salmon that Graham had stuffed and mounted and hung on the wall over the piano. The thing gleamed darkly against the birch wood Graham had on his walls.

Graham stopped fiddling around on the piano and turned around on the bench.

"The chart isn't any good," Sidney said. It had cost him something to say it; his head was throbbing. Any little noise felt like an earthquake; the piano had been killing him. But, he figured, if he made the comment, then Graham wouldn't have to talk as much, trying to say it gently. There would be no discussion, and Sidney could go home.

"Not completely true," Graham said, picking up the chart. "From anybody else, I'd say this was exceptional. From you—" He lifted his hands. He wasn't impressed with it.

Sidney kept his eyes on the salmon. The pain in his head was so hot and so pressing that he could hardly see past it.

"Are you mad?" Graham asked.

"No," Sidney said. He was surprised that Graham should ask.

"You don't look real happy," Graham said.

It was no longer a matter of having to concentrate on the fish. Now he couldn't stop looking at it. And the one stupid little phrase of music that had been stuck in his brain for days now just kept going around and around, repeating itself. It couldn't have been more than five bars, and it didn't make the least bit of sense, but he couldn't get rid of it, and it was driving him out of his mind.

"What's wrong?" Graham was asking him.

"I've lost it," Sidney said conversationally. And suddenly, he didn't really care anymore.

Graham sat there looking at him. It took a massive effort of will for Sidney to drag his eyes off the fish and to move them to Graham's face.

"You're serious," Graham said.

Sidney said nothing. "I wouldn't have expected that of you," Graham said. "With the kind of things you believe, I'd think there wasn't any room left for superstition."

"What things?" Sidney asked, his own words echoing on down into the middle of his brain.

"C.J.'s told me some things," Graham said.

"Really," Sidney said.

"What's wrong with you, man?" Graham asked. He started to get up from the bench. Sidney had to blink to keep up with the movement, and he wished Graham would just sit still.

The door opened and Nancy came in. "Graham," she said, and it was as if she had started talking before she had opened the door, "I *told* you about that sack of—" When she stopped, Sidney had to look at her. "Hello, Sid," she said, and her eyes narrowed slightly. "Sit down," she said to him.

He meant to decline politely, having been quite comfortable in the corner. But things being as they were, he thought he might be better off doing as she told him.

"He hasn't got any color in his face, Graham," she said, and she came over and put her hand against Sidney's forehead. The hand was cool, but the touch was searing. "Graham, what are you thinking of? How long has he been out of the hospital? How long, Sidney?"

Sidney shook his head, and was immediately sorry he had. He put one hand out on the arm of the sofa. He was cold, and he felt slightly wet all over—wet and cold.

Graham was standing up, looking worried. "We'd better take him home."

"You drive him in his car," Nancy was saying, "and I'll follow you in the Bronco."

"I'm all right," Sidney heard himself saying. It sounded as if somebody were talking underwater. He closed his eyes, and he felt the room slip under him. And he knew he wasn't all right, and he knew he was scared.

"I have four children," Nancy was telling him. "I don't like to have to say something more than once." But he wasn't arguing anymore. Now he was just hoping they could get him home before he threw up or fell down the stairs or did some other totally undignified thing in front of them. He wanted his bed.

He was hoping Courtney wouldn't be there when he got home. She'd want to know why Graham had driven him home and why Graham had helped him out of the car. Graham had said, "Tell Courtney," and Sid promised he would, lying through his teeth.

But she was home. And as he came through the front door, she was standing in the doorway of the kitchen, her arms folded and her face scared. It was a nice, warm afternoon. He let the screen close behind him, and he left the front door open. Keeping the piano between himself and Courtney, he went over to the desk and opened the top drawer, looking for the checkbook and the bank statement and a pencil because he hadn't taken care of his money for months, it seemed like.

"Calvin's not coming for dinner tonight," she said.

That was a disappointment. He'd been looking forward to that, the voices of the others murmuring away as he lay on the couch. "But Susan will," he said.

"Did you talk to her again?" Courtney asked.

He looked at her stupidly. "Since yesterday?" she asked.

"No." He leaned on the desk. There was a pencil in his hand.

"I thought she told you she and Will were coming over Friday instead."

This is the twilight zone, he thought. "Who's Will?"

Courtney looked at him carefully. "You told me about him. I've never met him," she said. "When you ran into Susan at the Record Plant, yesterday, she introduced you to Will. He's the violinist . . ."

He couldn't imagine what on earth he'd been doing at the Record Plant. *Not exactly low profile, are you,* he thought, *showing up at a place like that.* He tapped the pencil on the desk a couple of times, trying to remember. Maybe she was confusing him with somebody else.

"You don't remember, do you?" she asked. It was no use lying to her now. He didn't remember. And it couldn't have been scaring her any worse than it was scaring him. She started towards the desk. "I'm going to call the doctor," she said.

He held up his hand. A fountaining anger surged up inside of him. "You will not," he said.

She stopped, and her eyes flashed at him. "You need a doctor," she said. "Something is *wrong.*"

"And I will take *care* of it," he said very distinctly. "All I need is a little rest, and then I'll take *care* of it. When I feel better, I'll *call* him."

"That doesn't make any sense, Sidney," she said.

He jammed the pencil back into the drawer. "Girl," he shouted, "I don't have to justify myself to you." He slammed the drawer and hit the desk. He put both of his hands down on the desk top and rested against them, straight armed, until he could get the anger back out again. His stomach had turned itself upside down inside of him, and the throb in his head was horrible.

He straightened up and turned around, expecting that she would be crying, and rightfully so; he'd never talked to anyone that way in his life before, certainly not to his gentle sister.

He crossed the room and lay down on the couch. *If you just keep breathing,* he kept telling himself. *You just don't want to let the breathing get away from you.* "I'm sorry, kid," he said. She hadn't been crying. She'd been looking at him as if he'd struck her in the face. "Just give me a minute," he said, and he closed his eyes. He felt the room slipping out from under him again, but this time it was all right, because now he was home, and now he was lying down. So he just went with it, slipped right away.

She sat in his chair and watched him sleeping. She wanted to call the doctor, but she was afraid of Sidney. If the rest of them had been coming over—but they weren't. They weren't because Courtney had invited Emily over here tonight, and Susan wouldn't be in the same house with her, and Calvin had thought it best to stay out of the way. It had been a terrible mistake— inviting the girl. Courtney had done it out of pity. Emily had called her three or four times, wondering about Sid, wanting to see him, worried. And there was always the chance that Sidney might want to see her.

Now she was coming. And Sidney was like this. Courtney got up, went into the kitchen, and moved around in it for a while, absently. Then she went in and picked up the phone and tried to call Emily. No answer anywhere. It was late. She was probably on her way over here already. Courtney felt off balance, off stride. She was going to have to wake Sidney up and explain things to him, but she didn't want to do it yet, not until she was sure Emily couldn't be intercepted somehow.

More puttering around the kitchen. More calls. One to Calvin. He wasn't home yet, either. Courtney wrote the doctor's number out on an index card with a marker so that she could see it across the room.

One more call to Emily. No satisfaction at all, and the evening was coming on. Courtney sat down on Sidney's chair again. "Sid?" she said, and her heart was pounding. He didn't stir. She touched him. "Sidney?" He sighed. "I have to talk to you."

He opened his eyes and stared at the ceiling. "Are you awake?" she asked. "Yes," he said indistinctly.

"I've done something without asking you, Sidney. Please don't be mad at me. I was hoping it would be a good thing."

He frowned, not as though he were angry but as if he were trying to understand. He didn't move his head. "I asked Emily over here tonight."

He closed his eyes. "What?" he asked.

"I invited Emily over here tonight."

He turned his head to look at her, wincing. "*Why?*" he asked.

"She just got here from school, and she's been calling me. Sidney, she really wants to see you."

He went back to staring at the ceiling. "I don't want her in here," he said.

"She's going to be here any minute, Sid. I want you to make sure that's the way you really feel, because if I send her away this time, you know that's going to be the end of this one."

"I don't care. I don't want her in this house again. You should have talked to me first."

"You don't want to give her a chance to talk to you?"

She could see the line of his jaw go tight. When he spoke, his voice was cold and controlled. "I believe I have given her a chance," he said. "I threw myself right down on the ground in front of her just like Mom's cocker spaniel used to do, and she made an idiot out of me. I offered her everything I had, but none of it was good enough. She went ahead and did the things she wanted to do, and she expected me to sit around and wait till she was ready for me—"

"That's just not true," someone said from the doorway. Courtney looked up. The screen door opened and Emily came in, white faced and bright eyed, her cheeks crimson. She walked around to the far end of the couch because he wouldn't have looked at her if she hadn't gotten in his way.

"Isn't it?" he said.

"No. It isn't." She had her hands pushed into the pockets of her jacket. "I never said you weren't good enough. I always told you the truth, Sidney. I never told you this was going to work out. I told you there were things I had to have, and there were things I had to do. And I told you I was going to have them, and I was going to do them. I never misled you. I never asked you for anything. I never even accepted anything."

He glared at her coldly. "There were a few things you accepted," he said.

She started to say something else, and then she shrugged. "If it was me you loved," she said distinctly, "then you should have understood that what I am, I *am*. If I hadn't finished my degree, I would've hated myself and you for the rest of my life. If I'd married you outside of the Church, same thing. I know what I have to have. I know what I have to do. If it's *me* you want, then you have to accept those things, too. Everything has its price. If I have to lose you in order to be what I have to be, then that's the way it is. I didn't expect you to be here when I was ready. I just hoped you would be." She looked at Courtney. "I'm sorry," she said. And she left the house.

He hadn't moved. Courtney leaned forward and touched his cheek. He grabbed her hand as if she had stung him with it, and then, more gently, patted the hand and gave it back to her. He started to sit up, but he got hung up in the middle of the movement. He put both hands to his head and gritted his teeth. He lowered himself onto the couch again, and she saw there were tears on his face. She touched the tears. "Is this pain?" she asked him.

He wouldn't answer.

Fifteen

Sidney groaned. They were moving him and shifting him, and his head was roaring and wanted to split right open. "Don't," he said. "Dondondon't." Someone shushed him. He opened his eyes, and the light cut through them into the back of his brain.

"At least he didn't throw up in my Mercedes," someone was saying. He opened his eyes again, just a little. The walls were whipping by, white, white walls moving. It was Calvin he had heard.

"You're going to have to stay out here," another voice was saying now. The panic hit him almost at the same moment the knowledge did.

"Calvin," he said. Someone took his hand.

"I can't let you go beyond this point," the voice came again, cutting into his brain just as badly as the light had.

"I'm the man's clergy," Calvin said, "and his attorney. Unless you want to make some very expensive mistakes, I would suggest you forget that I'm here."

"Don't leave me," Sidney begged. The words didn't come out of his mouth the way he meant them to. The voices had all but disappeared into the noise in his brain. The other hand tightened on his.

Courtney didn't know how long she had been sitting in this room. When they'd brought her here, hours ago now it seemed, she'd understood that this was going to be his room. But he wasn't in it yet, and she began to wonder if they'd put him in another one by mistake.

This was a big room with no bed in it. There was a place for a bed, and then there was a sort of curtain that was drawn back, now, against the wall, and then there was this chair she was sitting on and a table and a few other chairs. *The room is big enough for two beds,* she thought.

Beyond the window, there were a few leaves; and there was Los Angeles, dark now. For the second time in as many weeks she'd called her mother with bad news, and her father also—and, of course, she had frightened them, because she was so frightened herself. And now she'd been sitting here for hours, cold and unable to feel her own hands.

Someone came in and turned on a light. A nurse. And then Calvin came in, looking tired. *Don't tell me he's dead,* she thought. She waited. Calvin pulled one of the other chairs up close to hers and took her hand.

"What?" she asked, her voice quite dry.

"I didn't want to leave you so long," he said gently. "They had to take him into surgery. He's been bleeding into his head all this time. They had to relieve the pressure. It was kind of an emergency."

Still, she waited. "You know my friend Roger? The one I go home teaching with? He came and we gave Sidney a blessing. I have that right, Courtney, to use the power of God to heal."

She looked at him.

"I think he's going to be all right," Calvin told her, putting his hand over her cold ones. "That's the feeling I got." He really believed that, that he had the power to heal. And at that moment, she saw no reason to doubt him. "They're bringing him up pretty soon." He still had her hands. He put his other hand against her cheek for a moment.

Someone else came into the room. Another nurse. This one came up and stood aside quietly, waiting for them to finish their talk.

"I'm Lee," she said. "You're Ms. Soloman?" Courtney nodded. "We're going to be bringing him up here in a moment." The nurse was studying Courtney. "You're welcome to stay, but you have to understand that this room has to be kept very quiet. He's going to need all the quiet he can get." Which meant, if you're going to get hysterical on us, this is neither the place nor the time.

Other people were coming in, setting up equipment, moving around the room. The quiet efficiency was nightmarish to Courtney, but she looked at Lee, and she nodded. "I understand," she said. And she did.

Then the bed came in. Sidney was no more than a shape under the white blankets. More movement in the room—bottles set up, machines moved into place. "If you'd like to come over here, I can explain some of this to you," Lee offered. "You can keep an eye on things for us while you're here. He seems to be responding very well, but we'll be coming in every fifteen minutes or so for a while, checking his vital signs. Don't let it worry you."

The nurses began to leave. Courtney and Calvin stood by the bed, looking down at Sidney. His right temple was still badly bruised. They had turbaned him with bandages.

Calvin put his arm around Courtney and pulled her head against his shoulder. "The worst is probably over," he whispered.

The door opened behind them, and the doctor came in and stood at the other side of the bed. "Courtney," he said, nodding in greeting, "it's been a long day." He turned Sidney's face slightly with his hand, looking at the bruise. "He nearly killed himself, you know."

Courtney nodded.

"Well, I think we got to it in time. You see here, where we've got this bruise? Around back here, there was a kind of internal bruise, a bleeder. It's not the kind of thing that shows up right away. If he'd called me—I assume he had problems. Headache? Loss of vision? Maybe a little loss of memory?" Courtney was nodding. "Yes, well, it's a fairly classic case. We could have caught it earlier. We made some little bur holes in his skull here to drain things. He's going to have an incredible headache for the next little while, and there may have been some damage to the brain tissue, but we won't know that until we can get him up and going a little bit."

He looked at Courtney. He looked at Calvin, and Calvin looked down at Courtney. He nodded to the doctor. "He has good, strong vital signs. I don't think we have much to worry about. But I want you to understand—ultimately, the whole thing is up to him. We can't heal the body; the body has to heal itself. We just do what we can to help. If he's fighting with himself in there, or if he gets depressed on us, then we can look for some problems. So you keep a good face on, will you?"

Courtney looked up at him and smiled faintly.

"And get some rest," Dr. Moody went on. Then turning to Calvin, "You make sure she gets rest."

Later on, they brought a cot in for her. By then Calvin had gone. He came back after half an hour or so, dumping a sack of hamburgers and a sack full of books in her lap. One quick kiss and he was gone.

She was alone in the room. She thought maybe she might cry, but then she thought that might not be wise. It had been a tense couple of weeks, and she was still holding all those anxieties inside. "I'm a time bomb," she thought. What might happen if the control broke, she wasn't sure.

She took the books out of their bag. They were strange books to choose for her, Burroughs and L'Amour. She was too tired and too hyper for the cot, so she curled up in one of the chairs and began to read.

It was so quiet. The nurses did come in every fifteen minutes or so. Courtney was cold, sitting there in the chair, but she was too tired to move. Sometime in the middle of the night, the time between nurse's checks lengthened. He was doing better. Even so, the hours were long and cold and strange.

Courtney had fallen asleep in her chair, *The Daybreakers* on its face in her lap.

"Courtney," someone said. The voice was alarming, not so loud for conversation, but raucous in this place. She opened her eyes and straightened up painfully in the chair. It had been her mother's voice, and it was indeed her mother who had spoken, standing there holding the door slightly open as if she were not sure she had the right room. "Is he in here?"

Courtney hushed her gently and pointed to the bed.

There was a muffled exclamation from her mother, who immediately went to the bedside.

"What happened?" she asked, her whisper strained. "You didn't really explain it to me when you called."

"There was some internal damage that didn't show up right away."

"What kind of a doctor has he got?" her mother whispered fiercely. "Sending him home before he knew for sure."

"It wasn't the doctor's fault," Courtney said quietly.

"Of course it was the doctor's fault," her mother declared, then caught herself and whispered.

"Mother, it wasn't the doctor's fault. It was Sidney's fault. Sidney walked out of here because he didn't want to be here anymore. The doctor couldn't do anything about it."

"He could have kept him here. Sidney is reasonable."

Courtney put her hand on her mother's arm and pulled gently. "Come on," she said. "Let's sit down."

She led her mother to the table. "Sit down, Mom," she said. Her mother was standing there looking at the bed. "He's resting. There's nothing you can do but stand there, so you might as well sit down."

Her mother sat, her face troubled, resigned, tragic, dignified.

"Oh, Mother," Courtney sighed.

"He could have reasoned with him," her mother said again.

"Sidney wasn't listening to anybody, Mother," Courtney said.

"Sidney is an angel." Claire put her purse down, taking her jacket off. She was wearing white jeans. She picked up Courtney's book, looked at the cover, and put it down again with only the slightest lift of an eyebrow.

"Sidney is an angel," Courtney agreed. "But he still wouldn't listen. He's been having kind of a hard time, and it's made him stubborn." She was reluctant to tell her mother any more than that.

"You never told me he was having a hard time," her mother said.

"It wasn't for me to tell, Mother," Courtney said.

Her mother's face showed so little of her disappointment.

"He could have written to me," she said. "Well, I know why he didn't. And I know why he's had a hard time."

"Why's that, Mother?" Courtney picked the book up and put it down on the seat of the extra chair.

"You get into a cult, you ruin your life."

"Mother, Sidney is not involved in a cult. For goodness' sake!" The woman didn't understand, because she didn't want to understand. She already knew everything there was to know. "Not everybody's Catholic, you know."

"I know that, Courtney," her mother said, using that I'm-not-completely-stupid tone. "But there's a difference between reasonable religion and being a fanatic."

"And Sidney is a fanatic?"

"Does a normal person run off and leave his career and his family for two years? I've read a number of books about this. There are some very strange things involved here, and I don't know how Sidney ever let himself get sucked into it. All *I* know is, it's made a stranger of my son."

Courtney couldn't try anymore. She always felt big handed and big bodied around her mother. It was stupid, but that's the way she felt, unable to maneuver. It was useless to argue.

"You haven't even asked about Eddie and Elaine," her mother pointed out.

Courtney stared at her, caught herself, and said, "I guess I wasn't thinking."

The absent look and the raised eyebrows said it wasn't the first time.

"How are they?" Courtney asked, although it had to be understood that for one of the few times in her life she really didn't care.

"Eddie hurt his back playing golf last week," her mother said.

Courtney murmured her sympathy, wishing she could pick up the book again, and then hating herself for the feeling. But her mother went on; Elaine was an excellent student but she had one teacher who . . .

An hour went by. The nurse had come again, casting a suspicious eye on the two women, leaving conditions for them in the air behind her as she left the room.

Later the door opened again. Claire was talking, so they didn't hear anything.

"Maybe I shouldn't have come?" a voice said, loud and thin.

The two women jumped, and then Courtney's mother turned and flashed, *"Morrie!"* jabbing her finger towards the bed in the shadows.

Courtney's father covered his mouth with his hand and hunched up his shoulders. He half tiptoed over to the table.

Courtney's mother sat staring at Courtney, seething with indignation, assuming her daughter's corroboration.

"Hello, Daddy," Courtney said. She said it with more than usual warmth, forgiving him for the loud voice. When she looked at her father in this light, he seemed smaller than he really was, and older.

"Is he all right?" Morrie asked, whispering now. He pointed at the bed. "Is it okay . . . ? I came as quick as I could."

"You didn't have to come," Courtney said to both of them. "I didn't tell you he was dying."

"Is he?" her father asked.

"I don't know," Courtney said.

"Can I look at him?" Morrie was peering into the shadows around the bed.

"Yes, come on," Courtney said. She got up and took his arm, and they walked over to the bed.

"Has he talked to you?" Morrie asked.

Courtney shook her head. Her father patted her hand, then he put his hand on the back of her head and, pulling her near, kissed her on the forehead.

They stood that way, looking down at Sidney, for a few moments in the silence.

"He looks like such an angel," Morrie said. He touched his son's cheek. "David himself could have been no more beautiful than this. So, he's been like this since you called?"

Courtney nodded.

"He'll be all right," her father said, patting her hand again. "I guess we should go sit down." He said it with such reluctance that Courtney had to smile.

"So, Claire. How is Eddie?" Morrie asked. He sat down and then stood up again quickly. He picked something up off the chair. "Your book?" he said, offering it to his ex-wife. She looked at it with immeasurable disdain.

"It's mine, Daddy," Courtney said, retrieving it.

"Since when do you read trash like that?" her father asked good naturedly.

"A friend gave it to me," Courtney said. "And it's not trash."

"So," her father said. He looked at Claire. "If I'd known I wasn't needed, I would have stayed in Chicago with my family."

"These children are your family," Claire pointed out bitterly.

"That's what *I* always thought," Morrie said.

"Meaning what?" she demanded. "Meaning what? That you have a right to be here and I don't? Is that what you're saying?"

"Is that what I said?" Morrie asked Courtney, his voice innocent. Courtney began to say something, but her mother cut her off. "Oh, Courtney's *always* been yours. Your little girl this; your little girl that. But Sidney's *mine*."

"Sidney doesn't *belong* to you, Mother," Courtney said, still whispering while the others were not.

Claire turned on her daughter, but Courtney wasn't looking at her. "Or to you either, Dad. We don't *belong* to you. We're your *children*, not your *weapons*."

"Tell your mother," Morrie directed.

"And where were you when these children were growing up, Morrie? Tell me that. Where were you when they needed clothes, when they had problems? I'll tell you where. Running around— that's where."

Morrie tossed his head sideways, rolling his eyes. "You want to know why?" he asked, leaning forward slightly.

"It doesn't matter *why*," Claire said, loudly, angrily. "What I'm telling you is you have no right telling me I don't belong here. *You* don't belong here. *You* walked out on them. *You* don't belong here."

Courtney hadn't heard the monitor for hours—it had been so regular, so unobtrusive. But now she heard it in the midst of the fierce whispering because the rhythm had quickened. Whether this was a bad thing, Courtney didn't know. One thing for certain, Calvin believed in some power he had left working on Sidney, and this room couldn't hold sanctity and hatred at the same time. This was all the stress she needed to blow the cork right out of her bottle.

"Will you *stop*?" she hissed. She was standing up, a mama lion, a junior fury herself. "He's lying over there in that bed. He could be *dying* and all you can do is bicker? The only thing you can think about is *yourselves*? Then you get out of here, because we don't need you. Either of you."

She burst into angry tears and pushed her face into her palms. "You're the most selfish people I've ever known," she whispered. She took her hands away and glared at her mother; both of her parents were just sitting there, staring at her. "Sidney doesn't belong to you, Mother. And you don't really want him. If you wanted him, you might just take *one* little minute of your life and listen to the way *he* feels about things. If he'd *told* you he was having a hard time, you wouldn't have heard it. You would have been too busy counting the pages in his letter to see if he'd written you enough. Sidney's a human being. So am I. I don't think you ever noticed that. Well, you can both just stop fighting over us, because we're on our own now, and I like Sidney's idea about God a lot more than I like yours."

She walked around the table and headed for the bathroom. "We could have been friends, all of us," she said, and then she shut the door on them and sat in the corner and cried herself out.

"And we're selfish?" she heard her mother say. Courtney sat in the corner, wiping her eyes with a tissue. She leaned her head against the cool tile, and she felt foolish. The anger, she put aside. It hadn't done anybody any good.

She stood up again and opened the door. Her parents were just as she'd left them, except that they were no longer fighting.

Courtney sat down in her chair again. "I'm sorry," she started to say, but her father put his hand on hers and pursed his lips, shaking his head.

"You had a right," he said. He patted her hand. "I apologize to you. From now on, everything we say here, we'll be sure to be nice. And we'll be sure to be whispering. Okay? Can everybody whisper?" He was looking at his ex-wife.

Her mother, still silent, handed Courtney a Kleenex. Courtney wiped her eyes with it even though they were dry now.

"I know there had to have been happy times," she said, whispering herself. "Or why would you have gotten married in the first place?" She looked at them. "Can't you remember any?"

Claire was putting things to rights in her purse. Morrie sat back in the chair and looked thoughtful.

"I can't believe you can't remember any," Courtney said. She wadded up the Kleenex and threw it at a waste can in the corner. It made a muffled sound when it hit.

"Not if you keep whispering at me," her father said.

"Well, how did you meet, then?" Courtney asked.

Morrie raised his eyebrows and looked at Claire, grinning.

"He stole my cab," Claire said quietly, still working with the purse.

"She was *in* it," he said. "You remember that? First I told him, Spring Street—that's where my maternal grandmother lived, on Spring Street—and then I got a good look at you, and I told him, Newark. Newark—can you believe that?" He started to laugh, and then he remembered his quiet son.

"You must have liked him." Courtney looked at her mother. Claire shrugged.

"She liked me," Morrie said. "She used to tell me I was impulsive. And she used to say, 'Morrie, you're so *forceful.*' " He chuckled to himself. And then he looked at Claire. "And your mother was the prettiest thing I ever saw. She was a Catholic, you know. I caught it for that with my grandmother. She still is . . ." He was looking at Claire.

"I'll always be a Catholic," Claire told him stiffly.

"I meant pretty," Morrie said. Claire looked at the table and drew herself in. "I'm sorry," he said. "I shouldn't have baited you." Claire shrugged again. "Maybe the thing still hurts," he said. "I try to make it all your fault. Even now I do that."

Claire looked at him. "Was it all my fault?" she asked. "What Courtney said to me, is that what you all think?"

"It takes two," he said. "We should be friends for them at least. We could do it. If we shut up, we could do it. All we have to do is say, 'it was my fault,' 'it was my fault,' and then, 'it's good now for us both and that's good.' Then we could be friends and not fight over our grandchildren."

Claire spoke to the table. "I don't know how to be your friend, Courtney," she said.

"Give me another Kleenex," Courtney said. Claire picked up the purse again. "All you have to do is stop expecting things," she said. And then she added quietly, "I believe, when you give yourself in love to other people, you don't have to worry about yourself."

Claire snapped the purse shut. "I'm tired," she said.

"You want me to take you somewhere?" Morrie asked. "I rented a car."

Claire looked at him for a long minute. "All right," she said.

"We could get something to eat. I make good money now," he said, winking at Courtney.

"All right," Claire said. She turned to her daughter. "Will you be all right by yourself?"

"Yes," Courtney said. "Just leave me the names of your hotels."

"We'll call you," Morrie said. He stood up. "You ready?" he asked Claire. She stood up and put her jacket on. "We'll call you," he told Courtney again.

"Okay," she said. She walked them to the door and stood there, watching them walk down the silent hall together. She was thinking it must be nearly morning.

She stepped back into the room, letting the door close slowly behind her, and she stood there for a while beside her brother's bed, looking down at him in the dim light. "Let him be well," she prayed. "Let him be whole."

She touched his hand. He stirred.

"Sidney?" she whispered.

He took a long breath. She took his hand in both of hers.

He sighed. "They go?" he asked. He slurred the words heavily. "Was it a dream?"

"You heard the folks?" she asked.

"They were here," he said. "I didn't know I was dying."

"You heard me say that," she said, kicking herself for the slip.

"I'm not dying," he said, drowsy and inarticulate.

"I know," she told him.

"I just *feel* like it," he added.

"Can I get you anything?" she asked him, but he had gone back under again.

She stood by him another moment, watching him. She put his hand back on the bed gently. *Go to it, Calvin's power,* she thought. *If faith helps, I'll have faith.*

Sixteen

He wasn't looking down on the surface of his thought the way he'd always done. Caught in some long, strange dream, Sidney had somehow gotten down inside the actual operating system, down below the surface of the finished thought to where all the things were sorted out and put together. And there was music down there; he was looking around and the music rose up all around him—sounds with trunks like trees, glowing sounds that flashed by like bright water, a sea of music, bubbling up from some place further down, a place he couldn't see into for anything.

And there was pain down there, too. He knew it was there, because he could see it all around the periphery, and it was pressing in, dark crimson and quiet. It didn't bother him at first. He was watching the music and trying to remember something. But the crimson tightened and pulled itself inward, encroaching on the music, coloring everything, gradually, gradually, until all at once it was the only color there, and the pressure of it was too much for him to bear.

And then he would have to open his eyes, and the light would burn them and someone would be talking, and sometimes it would be Sidney himself. He had seen Courtney there. Every time it came to this, and he could keep his eyes open long enough, he would see her. And every time he would tell her to go home, because he knew he had been crying out, or weeping, and he didn't want her there where he had to worry about her, too.

But she didn't leave. And each time he saw her, he was glad she hadn't gone. He didn't want anybody giving him his way anymore; he could no longer abide the consequences.

After a time, the music began to fade, or he had forgotten how to get down inside, and the crimson on the outside was not as intense. He spent more time with his eyes open, a waking dream with much confusion. But that began to clear itself away too.

He thought he had never met anyone as cold and efficient and heartless as his nurses were. There was a young one in the day, and she would shift things and make him speak and turn him over and have no pity whatsoever. And then there was the day when she turned him and gave him the shot in the hip, the one that was the awful pinch and burn. And when he yelped, she said only, "You must be feeling a little better, huh?"

He told her that he didn't want that shot. He wanted the old one, the old one that didn't hurt and that put him to sleep. And she told him that the old one and the one she had just given him were the same shot. And she expected him to believe it.

The night nurse told him the same thing. And they wouldn't listen when he told them he didn't want it. And every time he saw the nurses come in, he worried that they were going to hit him with the needle again.

But Courtney was still there, and that helped. She was always hovering, asking him what he wanted. In the beginning, he never wanted anything. Just to be left, floating slightly outside of reality. Sometimes they all came, all the friends, and they sat around in the chairs, talking while he idled—Altiri's freezer had gone out; Miri's little old niece had come to stay; the storm had thrown strange things up on the beach two nights ago—things that spun themselves into little dreams, and then he would drift back to sleep.

They started trying to get him to eat things, jello and yellow pudding and sherbet. They told him they'd just love to put him on oral medication if he would just start eating. But he didn't want to. His head still hurt. It ached. And when he coughed, it screamed at him. But it wasn't as bad as it had been; he could see past it now.

He had an argument with the night nurse over the stupidity of waking a man up so that he could be given a shot that would put him to sleep. She told him even night nurses had to have a little fun. He hated her.

Courtney explained to him that they'd had to shave part of his head. He couldn't feel it because everything up there was covered with bandages. He got into watching "Sesame Street." He did his best to explain to the bishop that he really appreciated his visit, but maybe it might be a nice thing if no one else outside of family would visit for a while—just until his brain cleared. And then finally, one day, he woke up in the morning feeling just like a regular man.

"And how are we this morning?" the doctor asked, studying the chart in his hand cheerfully.

"I can't believe you really say that," Sidney said.

"Well, I only feel as good as my patients feel," the doctor said, starting to remove the turban.

"He's got a cough," Courtney said from the other side of the bed, "and he feels hot to me."

"We've got a little temperature going here," the doctor agreed. "I wouldn't worry about the cough. It's just something that comes with the anesthesia. But we do . . . ," he was perusing the back of Sidney's head, "have a bit of an infection going in these bur holes. So"—he turned to the nurse and gave her some instructions.

"Now," the doctor said, "let's get you up out of that bed for a moment here, Sid." Sidney looked at him suspiciously. The doctor pulled the covers off and made Sidney sit up. "Up," he said. Sidney slid out of the bed and would have gone right on down to the floor, except they had been prepared to catch him. "Like a man," the doctor added. Sidney glared at him sourly. "Can you walk?"

Sidney took a step with his right foot. But the left one wasn't coming. "You've got nothing at all?" the doctor asked. "Come on. You've got good reflexes there." Sidney pulled the left foot forward.

"Is it all right if I throw up?" Sidney asked them politely.

"You don't have anything in there to throw up," the nurse said.

The doctor told him to get back in bed. "Your hands," the doctor said. Sidney gave him the right one. Everything was fine with the right one. Sidney gave him the left one.

"Hmmm . . . ," the doctor said. "Okay. You feel this? How about this? Make a fist for me." He put Sidney's hand back on the bed. "You work with it a little, and you'll get it back. You're just a little slow there. You start eating and get your blood going, you'll be fine."

The doctor walked out into the hall with Courtney.

Sidney lay there in the bed, cross and bored and nervous about his hand. "I want to go home," he told the nurse. She smiled to herself. "Then eat," she said. "Are you going to give me a shot?" he asked her, putting as much warning into his voice as he could. The question still came out more like a whine.

"Not right now," she said. He hadn't really looked at her before. She had nice eyes. Nice spice eyes. For a nurse. Her name tag said "Lee." She smiled at him. The smile was patronizing. Then she left. He watched her go out of the door.

Courtney came in. "You'd better start eating," she said. "They want you out of here."

"Okay, big boy. Time for a shower." Lee, the nurse with the spice eyes, pulled Sidney's covers off. He was indignant.

"I don't want to take a shower," he said.

"You need a shower," she told him. Courtney was across the room, sitting in a chair, reading, and she didn't come over and help him out at all.

"I don't stand up well enough," he pointed out.

"That's why I'm here," Lee said. She grinned at him. It was insufferable.

"No way am I going to take a shower with you," he said.

"Can you stand up?" she asked.

"You bet I can," he said.

"Not today," she told him. She was still grinning.

"You can't carry me," he said, folding his arms.

"Fine," she said. "Turn over." This he was used to doing. He turned half over, and then he said, "Why?"

But he already knew why. She'd pulled all the ties on the

gown loose. He dropped onto his back and held on to the gown with both hands. "What are you *doing*?" he demanded.

"If you won't take a shower, then I'm going to give you a sponge bath," she said. "Those are the alternatives." She had to put her hand over her mouth because she was laughing at him. If she hadn't been so nice-looking, it wouldn't have been so bad.

"This is funny?" he asked.

"You make such a big thing out of it," she said. "Look, I've already given you a couple dozen baths. I'm a *nurse*," she said.

"Not while I was awake, you didn't," he said. "And anyway, I've got this," he held up the arm with the IV attached, "and I'm a sick person. How can you torment a sick person?"

"You need it," she said. He wasn't going to win, and he knew it. "I won't pay for it," he said, a last ditch effort.

"Suit yourself," she said. She put out her hand. "Come on."

He sighed. "I won't look," she assured him soberly. Her eyes were laughing.

He lifted his hands, a gesture of resignation. "I'll probably throw up all over you," he warned her.

"That's okay," she said, helping him up. "Believe me, I'm used to it."

By the time they got back to the bed, the sheets had been changed, and Sidney was feeling a bit more fresh. Lee helped him back on the bed, and then she moved around, arranging things. He liked to watch her work.

"You should be using that hand," she told him. "Just even making a fist and opening it will help. How's your head?"

"Level one migraine," he said.

She frowned. "Really?" she asked.

"You're the nurse," he said as though she shouldn't have to be asking.

"That means I should know what's going on in your head?" she said. She leaned over him, pulling the pillow around under his head. He reached out towards her, and she pulled away from him quickly.

"I wanted to see your crucifix," he said, explaining.

She studied him for a moment, and then she leaned over and showed it to him. "My mother had one like this," he said, and then he let go of it. She gave the pillow one last yank.

"This one was my mother's," she said. "I wear it because I'm a Christian."

"Do you like being a nurse?" he asked.

"I do," she said. They had brought his lunch while he was in the shower. She pushed the tray over and lifted the cover off one of the plates.

"Lee, I can't eat that," he said. "I feel too queasy."

She looked at him sternly. "You feel sick because you're hungry," she said. "And that's probably partly why you feel so weak. Let me put it this way: do you want another Demerol shot? Or do you want to start taking some oral medication?"

"You're such a hard woman," he said, but he knew she had him. She put a plate of jello in front of him, little gleaming emerald cubes. "Isn't there some yellow pudding?" he asked.

"Just eat it," she said. He liked it when she smiled with her eyes. Bright cheeks. She had a sensitive mouth.

"Do your patients ever fall in love with you?" he asked, picking up the spoon.

"All the time," she said. She began to fiddle with the IV bottle. He put a spoonful of the jello in his mouth, and then he put the spoon down and took a little rest.

"Your sister says you're a pianist," she said.

He closed his eyes. A hundred years ago he'd played the piano. "I was," he said. The bed shifted under him. He opened his eyes. She was sitting beside him, and she put her hand on his.

"Look, Sidney," she said. "You have to understand; you're a very lucky man. You have a little problem. What happened to you was an accident. You can walk out of here and be anything you want. I know you're tired. And I know you've been hurting. But you can't lose your spirit. This is just a little moment of your life. Keep your perspective, and you'll get well before you know it. Let yourself get depressed, and you'll never get well."

He couldn't take his eyes away from hers. "Do you believe in God?" she asked. He nodded. "God will help you," she said. "Just remember that he loves you, and let him help. It's the best medicine in the world." She stood up. "Shall I leave the tray?"

"Leave the jello," he said. She pinched his cheek and gave him a saucy look, then she took the tray away. He was sad that she'd gone.

Later, when Sidney had fallen asleep, Lee sat down across from Courtney and smiled. "You should be a nurse," Lee said. "You have remarkable endurance."

Courtney laughed. "I do my complaining at home," she said.

Lee glanced over at the bed. "I'm a little worried about his attitude," she said. "He's such a lovely man. Doesn't he love somebody? I've never seen any girls in here besides you."

"He has a lot of friends," Courtney said, "but nobody in particular."

"That's such a shame," Lee said. "There's such a good energy in love. Actually, friendship should be enough. *You* should be enough. All it takes is caring about somebody else more than you care about yourself. I've seen love like that hold on to life so hard. He needs something to take his mind off himself."

"I know," Courtney said. "He has a mind of his own."

Lee laughed and stood up. "Tell me about it," she said. Lee wrote something on Sidney's chart, then left. Courtney couldn't help but think that Lee was right. Sidney needed something to think about.

Seventeen

"Would you like to add anything to this?" Courtney asked, handing Sidney the letter she'd been working on. He took it from her and looked it over lazily.

"Is this to Mom?" he asked, checking the first page again to make sure. "This is a nice letter," he said, as if he were proving a point.

Courtney had been fiddling absently with the tip of her dark braid. Now she tossed it back over her shoulder and sighed. "Of all the things I've messed up in my life," she said, "I figure my mother shouldn't be one of them." She was sitting in a chair beside the bed. He dropped his hand on her head and pushed her gently.

"What have you ever messed up?" he asked her.

"I haven't done *you* any good this spring," she said gloomily.

He gave one more push. "I would have died without you," he said. "Who else would have fed me?" And then, "You're not serious, are you?"

"I don't know," she said. "I guess I still feel guilty about school. It's just hard to know what's the right thing. But, I'll tell you something, Sidney. Things are starting to fall in line for me a little bit—"

"Then you, my dear, are doing better than I am," he said.

She sighed. "You're doing better than you think," she said.

"You've had some time to think about things. Don't you feel that maybe you should go back to school and finish?"

"No, Sidney. It would have been just as wrong for me to stay in school as it would have been for Emily to quit. Everybody's different. And you can't let anybody tell you what's best for you, because nobody knows better than you do what direction you have to go."

"You can't just do what you want all the time," he said quietly.

"No," she agreed, "but you have to weigh everything, and you have to make a decision for yourself. You have to learn to trust yourself. You can't let somebody else decide for you."

"Meaning me," he said.

"What?" She looked up at him.

"I'm the one who feels like you should still be in school, and I'm the one who wanted Emily to quit."

"That's right," she said. "You are. But I wasn't thinking about you specifically, just then."

He put his head back onto the pillow. "And you think I'm wrong," he said after a moment.

"I don't think you're *wrong*," she said. "But I think you're looking at things from your own perspective."

"But you think I'm wrong about Emily," he pursued, looking up at the ceiling.

"I think Emily has to have a chance to be what she feels she is."

"And I'm supposed to wait patiently."

"No," she said. "Nobody asked you to wait. You're not even in love with her anymore, Sidney. We both know that. You're just mad at the world. I think you and Emily could be friends. And I think you owe her one for the last time. You were pretty hard. Of course, you weren't exactly your normal self just then."

He picked up the pen and the letter.

"She's called to check on you." That was true. Emily had called once to check on him. "Maybe you should let her come and visit. You might feel better. I wouldn't want to think that I'd hurt somebody and never done anything to make it up to them."

"Think so?" he asked.

"Uh-huh." She stood up.

"Okay," he said, sighing. "Do you need this today?" he asked, holding up the letter. "Would you mind if I finish it later?" He put the letter down on the tray beside the bed.

"That's fine," she said. "Should I call her?"

"Why not?" he said. He groped for the buttons on the bed frame and lowered the head of the bed. "I'm going to go to sleep. Why don't you go do something interesting."

It had been so long since Sidney had understood what time it was. When his body wanted to sleep, his body slept — and that had been most of the time for the last many weeks. He never knew what time it was when he woke up, and sometimes he didn't even remember where he was. Then he'd see Courtney or Lee, and everything would be fine. The pain had gone to a faint, dull ache that was just as much in his stomach now as anywhere.

This could be hunger, he was telling himself as he came up out of a dream into daylight. Someone was standing by the bed, and he had to narrow his eyes down before he could focus on the face.

"Ahh . . . ," he said, screwing his eyes shut and then opening them again to clear them. "Little Red Riding Hood comes to visit the wolf."

She didn't say anything. When he looked at her again, it seemed as if her hair had caught all the light in the room. *Golden girl,* he thought. "Hullo," he said.

She was standing there, looking as if she was waiting for him to hit her. "We're not biting today," he said. "Come closer, my dear."

"Hello," she said, doing as he'd told her. "How's your head?"

"Much quieter, thanks." He smiled at her so that she'd know he wasn't just being flippant.

She looked down at the floor, and then she aimed those eyes right at him. "It's not like everything's just fine," she said.

He regarded her soberly. "Why don't we just forget it all," he said. "I'm going to be honest with you, Emily. I'm too tired for this. Let's just start over and just kind of . . . ," for want of better words, "see if we can't be friends."

There was a ghost of a smile on her face. "Come on," he said, wheedling it out of her. Her cheeks went pink. He'd always liked that. "Okay?" he said, chasing her eyes when she tried to look away. "Friends?" he said.

She shifted her weight and tipped her head sideways slightly. "Okay," she said.

"Okay," he said. He sighed a good, deep, drowsy sigh. "What's going on at the studio these days?" he asked.

"*Silversmith,* right now," she said.

"Hmmmm," he said. "There's a heavy duty band."

"They do all right on the charts," she said. She put her purse on the floor and sat down in the chair.

"How do you stand it, working around all these heavy teen idol rock dudes?" he asked her, grinning.

"I just control myself," she said.

"I'll bet you do," he said. She looked at him as if to say, we had an agreement here. But he was still grinning, so she did too. He got her to talk about school. It wasn't hard to keep her going, once she got started. He could just keep her talking and kick back and ride on it for a while. She was a nice girl. The interesting thing about it was, the more she talked, the more he realized he had a lot more in common with Susan than he had ever had with Emily.

Courtney came back from wherever it was she'd gone. She sat with them for a few minutes, and then she asked if Emily would mind staying for a while—Courtney had some things to do at home, but she wanted to make *sure* Sidney ate his dinner. Did Sidney mind if Emily stayed? No. Sidney was having a wonderful time. Would Emily mind? Of course not . . .

Then Lee came in to tell him she was going home. "It's the witching hour," he said dismally. Lee punched his pillow up and told him the night nurse wasn't so bad. A lot Lee knew.

It was so nice—one pretty blond girl sitting there to talk to, one very pretty lady in white, moving easily around his room, putting things to rights. Watching Lee made him feel warm and cozy inside. Emily was watching Lee, too. "Nice nurse," Sidney said. Lee turned around and smiled before she left. Emily smiled too. But it wasn't the same kind of smile.

"And then you had to do a paper on automation?" he said to Emily, getting her motor started again. She talked until dinner came, and then she made him eat it. All of it. Surprising what a forceful way the girl had. "Executive material," she told him prettily. And then she talked some more, and later they watched an old Gary Cooper movie on Channel 9.

He fell asleep somewhere in the middle of the movie, coming up every so often for a snatch of dialogue. The last time he came up, the TV was off, and the room was dark, and somebody was tucking him in. "Good night, Sidney," the somebody whispered, and he was sure it was Emily, because the night nurse would never have kissed him on the mouth.

He had very nice dreams that night. They had nothing to do with Emily, really. But they had everything to do with being kissed on the mouth.

There are dreams, and then there are *dreams*. And then there is waking up to the realization that someone is going to come before very long and give you a shower. Sidney made a herculean effort to get himself into the shower, all alone and quite private, before anyone else should come along and embarrass him any further.

"And where have *you* been," the pretty little nurse asked him as he came out of the bathroom, modest and right cheerful.

"I took a shower," he told her. "All by myself." Satisfaction all over. He refused her help and made his way over to the bed without fainting.

"Aren't *we* doing well," she said. "You're doing well enough that you'll be going home before you know it." Unaccountably, the satisfaction vanished. Here was something he had forgotten all about.

"I don't think I'm doing that well," he said. He was looking into those rich eyes, thinking he felt more like dying than going home.

"Come on," she said, tucking him back into the bed. "Don't you want to go home?"

"No," he said. She paused in her tucking, just a moment, just a breath, and then started up again. Courtney came in.

"Good morning," Courtney said. He, himself, was rather sour on the morning just now, and he thought she could have done with a bit less joy in the face. Lee had smiled at Courtney, but she wasn't smiling now. She finished tucking, then she checked the IV and left the room.

"How'd you sleep?" Courtney said, leaning over to kiss him on the forehead.

"Great," he said flatly.

"How was Emily?" she asked.

"She was great," he said.

The door opened and the doctor came in. "Morning, all," he said, picking up the chart. "Looks like you're on your way out of here," he said to Sidney. The doctor looked up and smiled. Lee and another nurse came in and started dismantling things. "You're eating well," the doctor went on. "Things look very good." He turned to Courtney. "Let's get him dressed."

And there were his jeans. "The nurse will give you a list of instructions," the doctor was saying. "If you have any problems, you call me, you hear me, Sidney?" Sidney hadn't heard him, but Courtney had. "Okay," the doctor said. "I want to see you in my office in a week." He left. The other nurse went with him.

Lee was taking out the IV. "Did I tell you?" she said, "I'm getting married next month." She slid the tubing out and held a cotton swab on his arm. "I've known him all my life," she said, deftly replacing the cotton with a Band-Aid.

"Congratulations," Sidney said, feeling as if somebody had kicked him in the stomach.

"I'll miss beating you up," she said. She smiled at him. The other nurse came in with a wheelchair. "You call me," the other nurse said, "when you're ready." She left.

"When you think of me," Lee said, "I wish you'd remember what I told you about God. I really do believe he loves each one of us. And I really do believe he's there when you want him." She smiled again. "I'm glad I met you. You too, Courtney," she said. And then she was gone.

Not too long after that, Sidney was tucked into the front seat of the old blue Volkswagen that Calvin's brother had loaned to them. The thing that was so devastating was that he should be so devastated.

"I called Emily, and I told her you'd call her when you felt better."

"Thanks," he said, looking out of the window. "You want to just plan on growing old together?" he said. "Just you and me."

"Sure," she said, laughing. "It shouldn't take too long."

"What?" he asked.

"Growing old. The longer I have you around, the older I get."

"Oh, *thanks*," he said. He sat there staring out of the window.

Finally, Courtney said, "Sidney, *every man* falls in love with his nurse." And he wondered if there had ever been another man in the world who was such a monumental jerk.

"Are you going to be all right?" Courtney asked gently. She'd put the car as close to the house as she could get it, but even that short walk had taken its toll on her brother's tiny supply of energy.

"You sit down," she said, pointing him towards the couch. "Will you eat some yogurt?" she asked. He didn't want it—she knew he didn't—but he smiled at her and nodded. He looked like such a waif—big, dark eyes in the thin face, his head still wrapped in bandages. The jeans he wore had never been really tight; now they hung on his body, bagging behind. He sat on the couch quietly, waiting for the yogurt.

"One of your studio session contractors called last week," she said as she came back into the main room with the carton of yogurt. She handed him the spoon. "It's always good to eat some yogurt when you're taking antibiotics." He seemed so fragile to her that she found herself mothering him.

"Which one?"

"Kenny Hodges."

"What did he say?" Sidney asked.

"He said he had a project that he had been holding off till you got home. And if you don't play it for him in the next couple of weeks, you're never going to work in this town again. I think he was kidding."

"He was kidding. So, what did you tell him?"

"I told him you were half-dead, and you'd call him when you could sit up."

He smiled at her. He had taken one bite of the yogurt and then had put it aside. "Good girl," he said.

"Why don't you go to bed?" she said. He looked so weary. He looked like somebody who'd been through something.

"I think I will," he said.

"Are you going to *stay* in bed this time?" she asked.

He smiled again. "I'm going to do everything you tell me to do," he said. "I promise." And it was true. For the next several days he did just as he was told, with a sweet, acquiescent absence of mind that Courtney found a little unnerving. What the doctor had said about damage had never left her mind for a moment, and now she began to wonder if Sidney was, indeed, all there.

Most of those days he spent in sleep. He ate moderately well. He walked around the house a little bit, watching the rain come down against the window, watching the tide come in, watching the sun set. Sometimes he sat out on the porch in the afternoon. He didn't talk much. It didn't appear that he was thinking much. But his face was beginning to fill out a little, and that was something.

Sometimes Courtney would sneak into his room after he'd fallen asleep and stand beside the bed watching him. In those moments she found that she loved him very much and that coming here had been a very good thing indeed. Whatever had been troubling her for those past many months was entirely forgotten now. Standing over him that way, she was at peace. But it would have been nicer if he'd been just the least bit stubborn.

_____Eighteen

The last thing his sister had said to him before she left that morning was, "Why don't you just stay inside and take it easy? I'll be home in a little while."

Well, he was tired of taking it easy. And he was tired of staying inside. He prowled around the house for a while, squeezing the little ball she had given him for his left hand. He thought about playing the piano, but he still had a headache. He was bored to death with tides and sunsets.

Sidney dreamed in music. Every time he fell asleep, there it was. And every time he woke up, it had gone, leaving no more behind than the memory of its having been there. A memory of a memory. He could conjure up nothing more—not a chord, not a snatch of melody. It made him cross and restless, and there wasn't anything in this house that was going to take his mind off his troubles.

So, he decided he was hungry, and not for yogurt. Yogurt was the essence of tedium. What he was after was milk and cookies—something with some character. He figured that Courtney had some cookies stashed away somewhere. He checked all the canisters, and sure enough, in the one marked Rice, he found what he was looking for. Keebler Pecan Sandies. With the slightest pleasant guilty tingle he took five of the cookies out of the bag and put them on a plate. Then he went to the refrigerator.

No milk. Such a disappointment. Such an injustice. There _should_ have been milk. He regarded his plate of cookies dismally. Alistairs next door probably have milk, he thought—if one of them is home. But then, another thought struck him: _What do you do when there's no milk and you want some milk? You go_ buy *some milk. You just go right on down to the store and you trade some of your money for some of their milk. Who could fault you for doing such a thing? Especially the people who had failed to provide you with your milk in the first place—they should have no problem with your doing that.*

It was such a pleasant idea—a little walk down the beach to Altiri's Market. A perfectly reasonable thing to do. But there was the matter of money. Courtney had the checkbook. Courtney also had all the money in the house. So he went into her room and poked around guiltily until he found a few dollars in a drawer. He stuffed it into his pocket. Then, remorseful, he found a piece of paper and wrote her out an IOU. He also found his house key.

Now that he was committed, he felt a certain urgency to act. Courtney had said she was going to be back soon, and Courtney wouldn't think highly of this idea once she was back home. He went into the front room and found one of his hats, the one that reminded Susan of Indiana Jones. They made him wear hats outside, now that the bandages were off; they didn't want him to get sunburned on his bald spot. That was fine—he didn't want anybody *seeing* his bald spot.

So, he grabbed the hat, put it on, gave the brim a tug, and stepped out into the wide, wild world. It was a dry, breezy sort of day, just as might have been expected in the end of May on the coast, and it felt to him as if it were the first day of the world.

He stepped down off the porch. Then he sat down abruptly. A little vertigo. *That's fine,* he told himself. *You moved too fast. Let's not be overanxious. One step at a time, here, easy as she goes—but get away from the house before somebody comes along and puts you back in it.*

He made it all the way past Susan's house before he had to sit down again. Once past Susan's—she was bound to take Courtney's view of things—he was in relatively safe territory. He was just a little shaky, just a little dizzy, nothing he hadn't expected. He had all day to get there, now. He sat for a long time, listening to the gulls. There were some people talking in a yard down the way; their voices drifted down to Sidney where he sat—drowsy afternoon music.

He got up again and stuck his hands in his pockets, kicking at a piece of driftwood that, another day, he might have tossed into the surf.

He was just beginning to think the whole thing might have been a terrible mistake, when Altiri's finally hove into sight—the justification, the thing triumphantly accomplished. He was hot now, and weak in the knees. He decided to take a little rest before he went into the store, so he sat down in the sand and lay back on his elbows, peering from under the brim of his hat at the fine broad ocean and the powdery sky.

There were sails out over the water, rainbow-colored sails— one crimson—moving lazily along. It was a good day for sailing; Sidney could see white horses in the waves. He took a deep breath and let it out easily, slowly. It was a good day for sailing.

And, sitting there quietly in the sand, he realized that some- how he had made peace inside himself. He was too tired to rage anymore. The wind came along from up the beach and tugged at his heaviness until it tore loose and blew away down the beach without him, leaving him high and dry on the sand behind, clear headed and open eyed. *What's the point?* he was wondering. *Everything here on this beach is in order, and it will be so no matter what happens to me. God's in his heaven and all's right with the world.* But he changed *world* to *earth* and felt better about it.

Everywhere he looked there was a crystalline immediacy, as if he'd just put on new glasses and things had finally come into focus. There was a crispness and vibrancy in the color and shape and movement of things he hadn't perceived for a long time. The act of *seeing* gave him quiet pleasure, and he took his time about doing it.

When he finally got up and went into the store, he knew he'd made a mistake in coming. His body was light and hard to con- trol, pushed too hard that afternoon. But he didn't care. He thought that as long as he was here he might as well get as much out of the moment as he could.

He was very careful about entering the market. Mike Altiri had no sense of humor at all. He kept the hat brim between his face and the cash register. Mike was too busy to notice him anyway. So Sidney drifted up the first aisle. They had just brought new bakery goods in; he could smell it. He lingered over the donut case, sorry he hadn't found more money. A boy came up and stood beside him, studying the donuts. Sidney glanced at the boy's face, thinking *he* probably had enough money. Something in the face caught his attention, some little thing, maybe just the fact that it was a human face with a life inside of it.

Sidney hadn't realized that he was staring until the boy started staring back. "Ummm," Sidney said. And then he back-pedaled, trying to explain that he'd thought maybe he'd known him, the face was *so* familiar. But probably not, huh? No, probably not. *The old brain isn't moving along real well today,* he told himself. *Now the kid thinks I'm some kind of weirdo.*

Actually, he *was* feeling a little weird. Nice weird. Light headed and happy. Silly, maybe. He wandered over to the dairy case, suddenly interested in eggs. Oh, and milk. And there was someone at the dairy case, too. *Busy day, Altiri,* Sidney thought. And the somebody at the dairy case was a nice, blond-haired, most pleasantly buxom young thing, who also was very interested in eggs.

Staring again. This, he could forgive himself, there was so much here that needed to be stared at. Of course *she* caught him staring, too. He felt the color come up in his cheeks, but for once, he didn't care, because she was smiling at him, and he had seen that look before. *She's looking you over, boy,* he told himself. *Oh, hold on.*

"Nice cheese," he said, conversationally.

She nodded. *Oh, speak,* he thought. Hair like gold, eyes as blue as the summer sky.

"Expensive, though," she said. She was grinning at him. *She thinks I'm on drugs,* he thought. And then it struck him that he probably was.

He wandered on, down through paper goods where there was a mother and a happy, round-faced baby. The baby was sitting up straight in the cart, trying to bite through an orange. He smiled at the baby, and the baby lowered the orange to smile at him. A funny, little almost-music danced around inside of him, and he passed on down the aisle.

He found a couple of little old ladies in produce, trying to wrestle some broccoli into a plastic bag. At first he thought it might be Miri and the niece he'd heard the others talking about, but that wasn't so. He stopped and helped them and managed to work the broccoli down into the bag without decimating either the bag or the vegetable. When they thanked him, he really couldn't distinguish one word from another. He just beamed at them and they beamed back, and everything was just fine.

And then he began to think it was time to go home. His eyes were beginning to get a little bit swimmy, or else his brain was. He stood still for a moment, trying to remember why he'd come in the first place. It was the milk. The milk. Over by the Nordic goddess. *Yes. Let's go over and get the milk.*

But the Nordic goddess was gone. Sadly, Sidney pulled the freezer door open and singled out a nice half-gallon, which, he discovered, required two-handed handling. He bumped the freezer door closed with his hip. Then, holding on to his milk, he went down the paper aisle to the cash register.

It was a sure thing he was going to catch it when Altiri saw him. Meanwhile, he stood in line happily, holding his milk, and making faces at the baby who was now standing in the cart in the line ahead of Sidney. In the line, there was the cart, and then there was a girl, and then Sidney. He stood just behind this girl, and he could smell her perfume. He made another face at the baby, and the baby laughed at him, one of those fine baby laughs that's a half crow. The mother looked up to see what was so funny, and the girl ahead of him turned around too. He smiled at them.

The girl was very pretty. All the girls were very pretty today. Bright eyed and bushy tailed and very, very interesting. The girl smiled at him. *Warms the old heart.* Then everybody went back to business, and they were just an old line again. He practically had his nose in her hair, beautiful chestnut stuff, cut a little like Courtney's. That's where the perfume seemed to come from.

He had meant to put his milk down on the conveyor belt, but somehow the room swung around under him and he missed the counter completely. The carton hit the floor with a sound very much like a ripe melon exploding, and the floor swung around the other way. Sidney threw himself back against the counter to keep from falling, and he hung there, trying to put the floor back down where it belonged.

Altiri was peering over the register. "What the—" he said. Sidney put one hand over his eyes so they'd close and clung to the counter with the other.

"Are you okay?" the girl in front of him asked. He opened his eyes again and the mother of the baby was watching him.

"Soloman," Altiri said, "What the devil do you think you're doing?"

"Thank you," Sidney said to the girl and the mother.

"Dimi," Altiri yelled, flagging down a skinny person in a butcher's apron. "We need a mop here." He leaned over the counter and looked down. He made a sound through his teeth. "What a mess!" He looked up at Sidney. "You want to explain to me what you're doing here? You can't tell me they let you drive yet."

"Susan talks too much," Sidney said. "I walked." The room still wouldn't straighten itself out. He crouched down and reached for the carton. The chestnut girl was just picking it up.

"Here," she said. Then he looked at her. *Looked.* He got stuck on her eyes.

"So, you're some kind of hero?" Altiri was saying. "Are you crazy? You should be home in bed and you're *walking*? What's wrong with your sister?"

It wasn't the color of the eyes, so much. It was something far more poetic. Windows of the soul. Her windows were open, and he'd fallen in through them, and now he didn't know how to get himself out.

"Are you all right?" she asked again.

"Would you *mind* getting out of there so we can clean this mess up?" Altiri said. The person with the mop came and stuck it right between Sidney and the girl. "The guy's nearly dead from a brain hemorrhage, and he's *walking*," Altiri said. "Okay, Mr. Hero. You get over there and put yourself on those bags of dog food and give me your checkbook. I'm going to call your sister."

Sidney absently handed him the wad of money.

Altiri said something under his breath. "Write it down," he said, handing Sidney a pen and a slip of paper. "Your *phone* number. Now *sit.*" Sidney left the line and obediently sat down on the dog food, the twenty-five-pound bags that Altiri kept stacked under the front windows. They made a lovely crunching sound as he sat.

The goddess had gotten into the line. It wasn't going to be bad, sitting here.

"When you get finished," Altiri said to the mopper, "go get Mr. Hero here another half-gallon." Altiri turned to the mother, holding the telephone between his shoulder and his ear. "I'm terribly sorry to make you wait," he said to her. "Sometimes we get crazy people and it makes delays." He finished her checkout, talking into the phone as he put the things into a sack.

The girl with the blond hair was watching Sidney. That was nice. He was watching her too. *I could do this all day,* he thought. But his eyes were hot, and he was suddenly very tired. He closed his eyes and kept them closed till they stopped burning. When he opened them again, the mother and the baby were gone, the chestnut girl was just picking up her bag, Altiri was off the phone, and Dimi was handing him another half-gallon, this one already bagged.

"I didn't have enough money for this one too," Sidney told him.

"Forget it," Dimi said, "You think he'd let you pay him?" Dimi took the bag away from Sidney and put it down on the floor. "Maybe you'd better not hold it, huh?" he said. He smiled at Sidney and left him there. The chestnut girl was gone. The blond girl was still watching.

He was hoping Courtney would come. He had this slow smile starting on his face because of that blond girl, and he wanted Courtney to get there before the girl got to him, because once that girl got over here it was going to be good-by dog food, good-by Sidney, forever.

And then there she was, standing right in front of him. *What a glorious dream I'm having,* Sidney thought. He sat on his hands.

"You need a ride?" the girl asked. *And what a nice voice you have, my dear. And wouldn't I just love for you to give me a ride.* Anywhere.

But he could see the old blue Volkswagen out of the corner of his eye. Hard reality came after him at last. "Thank you," he said, very pleased because his voice came out so low and husky, "but my sister's here." It came out like "my mother's here."

"Another time," she said. And visions of gourmet viands and after-dinner entertainment danced in his head.

"Undoubtedly," he said.

He carried the bag out to the car, handing it to Courtney before he got in. "We were out of milk," he said, not really believing it would make a difference to her, but giving it his best shot.

"Are you all right?"

"I'm all right," he said, and then he braced himself for the rest of what must come. But nothing further was said. She just started the car and drove home.

He slid down into the seat inside the seat belt, perfectly aware of the stupid grin he had on his face, but unable to do a thing about it.

"Thank you," he said. There was a lovely lethargic heaviness settling on him, and Courtney wasn't going to ruin it. "You're a very understanding woman," he said.

Courtney didn't say anything. She just smiled.

In the evening of that day Sidney took a couple of aspirin and fooled around on the piano for a while. Courtney and Susan had gone up to Miri's, and he had sent with them a respectful request that Miri start his lessons again as soon as she could stand it. His left hand was still slow, but then, so was his brain, and he couldn't see what good it was going to do, putting things off any longer. *It's about time we got on with this,* he thought.

He got up from the piano, restless again. He put on a jacket, zipped it up, and went outside to sit on the beach. It was a beautiful night, cloudless and bright with stars. The air was quiet. The peace that had come to him earlier in the day was still in residence. He made himself a nest in the sand, just where the dry beach crested and began to make its descent to the sea. After a moment he scooped out something like a shallow trough and lay back in it, the still sun-warm sand round and firm under his back, and the studded heavens inscrutable and beautiful above.

He was drowsy, lying there listening to the round waves breaking and rolling in. His mind began to wander. He found that he didn't really believe the stars were all that far off; he knew the truth of the matter, but he didn't *feel* that way about them. He began to wonder which star was God's own star.

And then he found himself asking, *Do You really have a star up there? Are You really there?* The little voice in the back of his mind laughed. *Such a question. You spend two years telling everybody in creation that God is real, and then you don't know yourself?*

It was a valid response. *Okay*, he thought. *Let's say I believe he's there. I hope he's there. How about that?* Then he began to wonder. *Do You really care that much about me? Did You know that kid was going to run into me? Did You allow that to happen or what? Did You make it happen? Why would You make it happen?* And then the little voice was saying to him, *He maketh me to lie down . . .*

Now, come on, he said to himself. *Okay, so you were wearing yourself out, and he slapped you a good one to make you quit it?* He laughed, thinking that if Miri could hear what he was thinking, she'd tell him he was crazy. "Sidney," she'd say with that sharp old voice of hers, "the Lord is *not* going to hit you with a truck just to get your attention. If you're not paying attention, that's your *own* problem."

He thought about that. And then he thought that Graham had been wrong; even after all the scriptures and the lessons and the discussions, there was still a lot of room for superstition. Where does the truth leave off and the folk religion start? He couldn't have said.

Okay then, he said to himself. *What do you believe? Does the Lord care how you feel?*

Yes. The Lord cares how I feel. I hope he cares how I feel.

Yeah, but—he apparently doesn't care if you die. Because death is insignificant to him.

Well, isn't most of this life going to be insignificant to him?

Okay, Sidney thought, directing his question at the stars in general, *do You care whether I can play the piano? It's significant to me, but is it* significant? *Did You put the music in my head in the first place? Where did it come from? Did You take it away again? Why did You do that? You want me to be happy, don't You? Or maybe the music shouldn't have anything to do with whether I'm happy.*

So, what should be making me happy? I don't know.

Okay, what about this one. Let's just say it's given: the music came from God. Okay. So, he gave it to you. So, let's say, he comes to you one day and he says, "Sidney, I want my gift back now." What are you going to do? Are you going to say, "Sure, here you are"? No bad feelings?

"Hooo," Sidney said out loud. "This is an ugly question."

And he wasn't sure he could answer it.

Don't you trust God? he asked himself.

No, he answered. *I don't think we think the same way.*

Doesn't he want you to be happy?

Yes, he does want that. That's what I believe. He does want me to be happy.

Okay, doesn't he know what's going to make you happy? Who do you think knows better, you or God? Sidney wasn't willing to give that one an answer right away either. Not an honest one.

Okay, who wants to live out eternity on a world that's a sea of glass without any trees or mountains or grass or anything? I don't, he thought. *But that's what you're working for, boy*, he told himself. It didn't seem right.

Do you think he's going to reward your best efforts, your righteous efforts, by taking away everything you love (and who taught you to love those things in the first place but he himself?) and replacing it with something you'll hate? Does that make sense to you?

That didn't make sense to him. *So, obviously, the Lord knows more than you do about what makes you happy.* "Okay," he said out loud. Now he was on faith. Faith was something he thought he understood. Or maybe it was hope he understood.

He heard Courtney drive in. "Gotta go," he told the stars. But he still hadn't answered the question, the Abraham question. And it hung on the night air behind him.

Nineteen

"She's really going to make me wait a week?" he asked. It was morning, and it was going to be a gorgeous spring day. Sidney, having taken a couple of aspirin, was at the piano. Courtney was in her kitchen, and all was well with the world.

"Miri said," Courtney called, "when you're well enough to go to church, you can start your lessons."

"Ahh," he said, and he began to play. He was playing the Bach piece, but he wasn't working on it. He played it through idly a couple of times, and then Courtney came out of the kitchen and leaned against the doorway.

"That's nice," she said.

He grinned. "Thank you. It's not, really."

"At least it doesn't sound like you're going at it with a jackhammer," she said. She went back into the kitchen.

"Jackhammer," he huffed to himself. Not really in the mood for Bach, he riffled around in his cabinet for something else. He pulled out his book of 60s tunes.

He flipped through the book, stopping somewhere in the middle of it, and he started to play. After a while Courtney came out again. "We're going to eat in a minute," she told him. "Are you reading that?" She gestured toward the book.

He looked down at his hands. "Not really," he said. "I'm just kind of fiddling with the chord changes."

"I thought you said you couldn't _play_ anymore," she said.

"Well," he said. "I can't."

"You _are_," she pointed out.

He played a funny little riff with his right hand. "Not really," he said. He paused thoughtfully for a moment. "It's like, I can feel what should happen from the outside in, but I can't really _feel_ it, you know what I mean?"

"No," she said. "You have two minutes till eggs."

He sighed. "Okay," he said.

He spent the whole morning at the piano. He still hadn't answered his own theological question. He'd tried to shrug it off this morning, but it had been following him around all day, hovering at the edges of his thought. But he hadn't wanted to think about it, because he *knew* what his real answer was and he was being a big coward about facing it. So he was cross most of the day. Courtney didn't seem to mind at all. She had this maddening mellowness about her that made him crosser than ever.

"Okay," he finally said, spinning around on the piano bench. She was sitting on the couch behind him, and had been reading a book. "I want you to tell me something."

She looked up.

"Okay, let's say that someone asked you for something. No, let's say that Dad asked you for something . . . and that . . . Okay, let's say, you know that he loves you better than anything in the world, and he'd never do anything to hurt you, because your happiness meant everything to him. Okay?"

"Okay," she said. She had the patience of a saint.

"Well, let's not use Dad," Sidney said, reconsidering.

"Why not?" she asked.

"I don't know. He's just not the right example."

"Why not?" she asked again.

"Because, what I'm after is something that's very selfless. The kind of love that isn't second to anything."

"And he's not a good example," she said.

"Not for most of our lives," Sidney said. "Okay, let's say *I* asked you for something. Something abstract. Something that meant everything to you. You understand? Can you think of something like that? That means more to you than anything?"

She didn't think very long. "Yes," she said.

"What is it?" he asked, suddenly curious.

She looked down at her book and colored up.

"What *is* it?" he asked, laughing.

She looked up at him, her eyes very bright. "My time with Calvin," she said.

"You're kidding!" he said. Never in the world would he have thought such a thing.

"No, I'm not kidding. You asked me."

"You're not in love with Calvin," he said. But she was, you could see that. She never looked prettier than when she was embarrassed like this. "*Calvin?*" he said.

"What's wrong with Calvin?" she asked.

"Well, nothing," Sidney said. "He's my best friend." He didn't feel so much like laughing anymore. "When did this happen?"

She shrugged. "All along," she said.

"I would never have known," he said. He was definitely not feeling as jovial inside anymore.

"You had things on your mind," she said.

He nodded slowly. "I must have," he said quietly.

"Sidney," she said. "I'm probably going to marry Calvin."

"Whoa," he said. It was costing him something, making the words sound as they should have. He was beginning to feel a little left out and hurt. "That's great. Does he know?"

"Yes, he knows," she said. She had one of those very stupid grins on her face, and she wasn't looking directly at him. Then she sobered up and looked at him, and he wished she hadn't. There was something in her face that scared him.

"There's something else," she said. "I wanted to tell you before, but there's never really been a good time . . ."

"What?" he asked. There was something unpleasant in his throat.

She took a slow breath. *Somebody's died,* he thought.

"I think I'm probably going to be baptized an LDS person before too long." She was studying his face. "And Sidney, I hope you forgive me, but if I do this, I'd really like Calvin to be the one who does it. Not because I don't love you."

If he had never understood the word *thunderstruck* before, Sidney now knew what it meant. His mind just stopped. His sister looked unhappy. "I'm sorry," she said. He still couldn't say anything. He looked away from her, and he laughed a flat, little stupid laugh.

"I knew this was going to make you feel bad," she said unhappily.

"I don't feel bad," he said. Of course it was a lie. "This is wonderful. You couldn't have said anything about it to me before?"

"I've started to talk to you about it before," she said. "But, like I say, you've had a lot on your mind. And, you know, you've been on drugs a lot lately."

He smiled a little bitterly. "Now, you're sure it's not just because of the way you feel about Calvin?" he asked.

She shook her head. "I'm sure."

So, he'd been sitting here in his house with his sister and his best friend, totally unaware of what was going on, all caught up in his own little problems, and somebody *else* has to do his teaching for him. *What else has she been going through that you don't know about?* he asked himself. *She could have cut off her left leg, and you wouldn't have noticed.*

"Sidney, don't *cry*," she said.

"I'm not," he told her. But he was. Because he was so angry. "Excuse me," he said. The bitterest part was, even now, he couldn't make things right with her because his own feeling was getting in the way. "I'm going to take a walk," he said.

"Where?" she asked. Now she sounded scared, as if she thought he was going to hurt himself.

"It's all right. I'm going to go sit in the sand," he said. "I'll just be outside." He stopped at the front door. And then he said, "I'm sorry, Courtney. It just strikes me that I have to be the biggest jerk in the world. You shouldn't have to be apologetic about something like this. I'm proud that my friend is the one you want. Please don't think I'm not. I just . . . ," but there wasn't any more for him to say. So he left. And he hoped she would understand, just this one more time.

"So, where's Sidney?" Susan asked. She was cutting up peaches in the kitchen while Courtney rolled out a pie crust. "Be careful," Susan admonished. "You're not going to want to work with it too much."

"Like this?" Courtney asked.

Susan slid down off her stool and picked up an edge of the crust. "Still too thick," she said. She picked up her cutting board

and put it down on the kitchen table so she could watch Court-
ney better.

"He's outside," Courtney said.

"Are you sure?" Susan asked. Courtney laughed, nodding.
"He promised he wouldn't take any more walks."

"So, what's he doing out there?"

"He's sitting."

"Is he mad or something?" Susan asked.

"I hope not," Courtney said.

Susan picked up the edge of the pie crust again. "You told him
about you and Calvin—and everything," she guessed, looking at
Courtney. "By the way, this," indicating the crust, "is about
right."

But Sidney was not actually sitting. He was pacing. And he
was calling himself all kinds of harsh names, most of them
embellished with such heartily descriptive terms as "stupid" and
"selfish."

The pacing couldn't last long. In the end, he did sit.

Well, you've lost something, he told himself, *and getting mad
about it isn't going to change anything. So, you might as well try
to salvage what you can. Now, how are you going to do that?
Maybe you should just stop worrying about yourself so much.
How about that for a start? Maybe you could take care of Court-
ney a little bit in the time you've got left. Maybe you could just
shut up because I'm totally sick of you.*

He looked out over the ocean and into the sky. *Whatever it is
I thought I had, You can have it,* he told the Lord. *I don't want it.
I don't want anything.*

"How'd you learn to do this?" Courtney asked, trying to peel
a layer of the pastry off the rolling pin.

"My grandmother was a great cook," Susan said. She licked a
drop of juice off the inside of her wrist. "When I make stuff like
this, sometimes I can remember what it was like, sitting in her
kitchen, watching her go at it. She always told me that good
cooking makes up for a lot. I don't know how she came up with
that little bit of wisdom, though—she never had to make up for
anything."

Courtney glanced at Susan. She put the rolling pin aside and picked up the pie tin. Susan dumped the peach slices into a bowl.

"So, is that good or bad about your grandmother? Like this?" Courtney began to lift the crust up off the table.

"Don't put *holes* in it, now—yeah, like that. Oh, my grandmother was . . . I don't know. She was one of those serene people. I always wished I could go and live with her. She had everything under control, a beautiful house, a husband who adored her. I used to pretend they were really my family. Her house was warm, you know what I mean? I used to want to be just like her."

"You don't anymore? This is going to tear when I pick it up."

"No, you fold it over. Okay—no. By halves. First—yeah, like that. Don't squish it, though. No, I still want to be like her. So far, I've blown it. I'm glad she died before I hit sixteen. I think she would have been real disappointed in me. She really believed in the traditional morality. She wouldn't have liked my world very much."

"Courtney picked up what she had made and set it into the tin. "Don't tear," she told the crust as she unfolded it ever so carefully. And it didn't tear. She smiled at it with great satisfaction.

"Good," Susan said, beaming. "You'll be a great cook yet." She dumped a cup of sugar over the peaches and began to toss them around in the bowl with her hands. "What are you going to do?" she asked. "You going to spend the rest of your life cooking for Calvin and having kids? Does Sid still want you to go back to school? Not that it matters much what Sid wants just now."

"I don't know. I'm not a cook like you. You have a real talent here, I think. I don't think I enjoy it as much as you do. We'll see. The nice thing is that I really don't think that Calvin *expects* me to do anything. I think he'll be happy with me however I am. He does like to eat, though. Maybe we'll go out a lot."

"Just as long as he doesn't expect you to cook," Susan said, dumping the peaches into the crust. "I *hate* men like that. My dad was like that." She wiped her hands on her jeans.

"Does Will expect things?" Courtney asked.

"It wouldn't matter if he did," Susan said. But her voice had softened. "I'm trying to make a friend out of him," she said. "It's about time for me to have a friend." She picked up the last bowl.

"You know, I've wasted a lot of time in my life. I wish I'd always been more like you."

Courtney looked at her. "No, Susan," she said. "It's *you* I love."

Susan looked down into the bowl and half-laughed. "You know, I love you too. You're more of a sister to me than my sister ever was. There's just so much I regret."

"Come on, buddy," Courtney said. "It doesn't really matter how things used to be anymore, anyway, does it?" She put her arms around Susan and held on to her. "Everything's kind of even now."

"You didn't happen to tell him about me, too, did you?" Susan said.

"Nope." Courtney planted a kiss in the middle of Susan's forehead. "I think that's for you to do. Anyway, I wasn't going to tell him another *thing*." She let go of Susan and started to wipe up the table.

"Really took it hard, huh?" Susan asked. She turned the water on and rolled up her sleeves. "Serves him right. He never thinks about anybody but himself lately.

Courtney squeezed the rag out thoughtfully. "Oh, I wouldn't say never. He's always been a sweetheart—it's just lately he's been a little confused, and it makes him self-centered."

Susan attacked one of the bowls. "*I* think you ought to get his head examined."

Courtney laughed.

"I'm serious," Susan said, her own laughter held back. "I think there's something wrong with him, and I think you ought to get some professional help, somebody who works with musicians or something. I really do. He's been like a manic-depressive lately. You can't tell me he's rational." She had just started to say something else when they heard the front door open. They looked at each other. Sidney appeared in the doorway. The two girls were still looking at each other, wide eyed and delightedly guilty.

"You're talking about me again," he said.

"What makes you say that?" Susan asked, and the two of them began to laugh.

"Oh, well," he said. "Oh, well."

"He was so *nice* to everybody tonight," Susan said to Courtney later, after Trivial Pursuit, after pie. "Will should have been here. Sidney might have made a good impression. He might even have noticed Will was *here.*"

Sidney had walked Calvin outside. They were standing out on the porch, just outside the door. "What are they *doing* out there?" Susan asked.

"Sidney's giving Calvin a hard time, I expect," Courtney said serenely.

"Okay, so maybe I *should* have talked to you about it first," they heard Calvin say.

"Is he kidding?" Susan asked.

Courtney sighed.

"It's a good thing you make good money, at least," they heard Sidney say. "You *eat* enough."

"He *is* kidding," Susan said.

"You know," Courtney said, "maybe this'd be a good time for you to talk to Sid. He's been in pretty good shape all evening. You should probably talk to him when he comes in."

Susan made a scared face. The screen door opened. "Just keep that in mind," he was saying over his shoulder.

"Keep what in mind?" Courtney asked mildly.

"I told him," Sidney said with great dignity, "if he didn't treat you right, I would bash his head in. And now, because I have a number of important things to do tomorrow, and as I am nearly nauseated from good news and good food, I'm going to bed." He held up one hand. "Please. Don't beg me to stay. I'm *sure* you guys have a lot to talk about." One quick sardonic smile and he was gone.

"Aren't *we* hilarious?" Susan said.

"Well, there goes your chance," Courtney told her.

Twenty

Sidney stood in the kitchen doorway, pulling on his dark linen jacket. "I'm going up to Miri's," he said.

Courtney was pulling groceries out of one of the brown bags that stood on the kitchen table. "Did you call her first?" Courtney asked.

"Of course I called her," he said. "I told her I was going to church Sunday, so she should let me come up."

"And so, you need a ride," Courtney said. It was a service she loved to render, and she hadn't meant to offend him with the offer.

But he stood up and put on his dignity again. "No, thank you," he said. "I'm going to walk."

Courtney put her hand on her hip and regarded him severely.

"I made it to Altiri's," he pointed out. "And this is about half as far."

"Straight up the cliff," Courtney said.

"I'm stronger than I was two days ago," he said. "If I faint, I'll call you."

"Are you in such a hurry?" she asked gently.

He sat down again. "You know," he said, and his eyes made it plain that she should try to understand, "every night I dream music. All night. And every morning—or sometimes in the night, because I wake up then, too—the music disappears, just the way the fog does when the sun hits it. It just sort of vaporizes. It's so _frustrating_ because it's so _close_," he said. "It just about makes me want to cry, sometimes—kind of like just missing a plane when somebody you loved was on it." He looked at her. "I need to play," he said. "I need to try."

She mussed his hair. "Maybe you shouldn't worry so much. Maybe if you didn't chase it, your music would come back to you on its own." She started studying the crown of his head. "This doesn't look so bad," she said, touching the shaved place where the hair was coming back in. She patted his shoulder. "If you faint, call me." She folded up one of the brown sacks. "Maybe you'll get to meet Miri's niece," she said. "She's a good lady. Call me when you're finished, because I want to come and get you."

I told her, he thought to himself. *I told* her I could do this. He was sitting at the top of the cliff, getting his wind and his balance back. It had been a long, slow climb. He'd taken off the jacket, and he was sitting there in his tee shirt, feeling the wind on his arms. The sun was getting down there towards the water, and the water was starting to take on a little vermilion where it met the sky.

He sighed, contented. *So,* he said to the Lord. *I guess what I said yesterday doesn't really count for much. I've been thinking about it. I think, if I have something, and if You want it—I think I'd better go ahead and give it to You. I don't know anything. And I think, if there's something precious to me, it would be safer in* Your *hands than in mine. So, I tell You, in all coolness of mind, no bitterness, no resentment—if there's something of mine You want, then okay. You have it. I'm not going to fight You. I'd be a bigger fool than I am to do that any longer. I've lost part of my sister's life. I don't want to lose anything else. So, there's my answer. That's my answer today, anyway. Just do me one favor? I'll give you everything, no strings attached. Only, keep a net out for me? I'm going to need it; I know I am.*

He stood up and made his way along the cliff's edge to Miri's cottage. He took off his hat—this one was more *Man from Snowy River* than Indiana Jones—and wiped his forehead with the back of his hand.

Miri met him at her garden gate. She was still wearing her wide-brimmed hat and was just pulling off her gloves. "Well," she said, "you don't look so bad." She put her hand under his chin and turned his head so she could see the side of his face. "Still a little bruised," she observed. "Well, you go on inside. This sun is too much for either of us . . ."

So, he found himself in the little hall between her front door and the parlor. The hall was cool and, to his eyes, so thoroughly dark that the warm coral light at the end of it seemed quite startling.

When he stepped into the parlor, he was confused; the light that came in through the windows was strong and bright, broken up into fragments by the trees outside, and tossed around on the floor as the trees themselves moved in the breeze. The play of the light made him dizzy for a moment.

There was someone else in the room, someone standing in the brightest light just in front of the windows. For a moment he couldn't tell if the person was male or female, or if he was seeing back or front, but he figured this must be Miri's niece, and he smiled politely, squinting into the light.

And then his eyes could see, and she came forward with her hand out. And it was someone he knew. It was the chestnut girl from Altiri's. It was, indeed, all the same—hair, face, and the eyes—he knew those eyes very well. He wondered if the perfume would be the same, too, and the thought of standing that close to her again made him weak in the knees.

"Hello," she said. "I'm Miri's niece, Virginia."

And he was standing there with his mouth open, forgetting to say anything. She gave him a funny little prompting look. He shook his head, as if that could clear it.

"Virginia," he said.

She nodded, smiling, helping him along. "That's *my* name. Yours is . . ."

That's what she wanted to know, of course. His name. Perfectly natural that she should ask. Only, he couldn't come up with it right away. This had never happened to him before. The only thing he could think of was Halliday, and that wasn't the right one.

"Soloman," he said at last, feeling about as stupid as he should have been feeling.

"The wise?" she asked, still smiling.

"Not evidently," he said. "I'm sorry. I just . . . I've seen you before."

"At the market," she said. He cringed, thinking of it.

"I don't make a very good first impression," he said, thinking he was getting a reprieve, and that he was still making a mess of it.

"No," she said, and her eyes were laughing.

"You've introduced yourselves?" Miri said from the doorway. "I'm just not quick enough these days."

"That's all right, Aunt Miri," Virginia said. "We've done all right. And it's Sidney, isn't it? Your first name?"

He nodded. "My aunt's told me a lot about you," she said.

He looked at Miri with grave misgivings. What did Miri *know* that she could tell? Miri shook her head at him, and her eyes were laughing too. "You're going to make him nervous, now," she told her niece.

He made himself smile at them. And then Virginia was smiling again. And then he was really smiling, and then he wished he could pull his hat down over his face. *Godzilla meets Snow White,* he thought. *Why did I ever think I'd grown out of adolescence?*

"We're out of milk, Aunt Miri," Virginia said.

Nooooooo, he thought. *Now she's mocking me.*

"Oh, I'm sorry," she said, understanding, "but we really are. So while the two of you are working, I'm going to go down to Altiri's and get some."

"The keys are on the hook," Miri said, starting towards the piano.

"I thought I'd walk," Virginia said. "It's so beautiful." And Sidney was still standing there, looking at her. There was a sweet wistfulness about her—something in her voice. Most arresting. Utterly disarming.

"It'll be dark before you get back here," Miri warned, a strong veto.

"I could . . ." He had spoken without thinking. *You could what?* he asked himself. *Faint on the way?* But the offer had already been substantially made, and he wasn't of a mind to rescind it. "I could go with her," he finished. "Then she wouldn't have to worry about the dark." He felt a need to explain it to them. To himself he thought, *And it's not like she has to worry about* you.

"You have a lesson," Miri reminded him.

"We could start next week," he said.

"No," Virginia said. "It's just a gallon of milk."

Miri was studying her niece. "You can't have pancakes with lemonade," she said thoughtfully.

"True," Virginia said, thoughtfully. "Or peanut butter sandwiches either."

"I really wouldn't mind," he said, wondering if he could make it all the way down the cliff and then to Altiri's.

"The lesson is important to you," Virginia said, looking at him out of those eyes. He thought it was a very insightful thing to say. So she was insightful, too, besides smelling so nice.

"I'm glad to be of service," he said.

"Okay," she said. "I've got to get my jacket."

She left the room, and he sat down on the piano bench. The corners of Miri's mouth were working away, as if she were holding something in. A laugh, perhaps. But he didn't care. All he wanted to do was get to Altiri's without making an absolute idiot of himself.

"Are you sure you want to do this?" Miri asked him. "You look tired."

"I *am* tired," he said. "But we can't let your little niece wander around in the dark all alone, now, can we?" he said.

"Well," she said, "that's very kind of you. Now, when are you going to want your lesson?"

"I'd rather not wait a whole week," he said, having found a whole new reason to enjoy the sights up here.

"Well, not tomorrow," she said. "Let's say Friday."

"Okay," Virginia said. "Let's get going." She looked at Sidney with amused suspicion. "Are you sure you want to do this?"

He sighed. "Yes," he said. "It's not that big a deal." Lies. Lies.

"You'd better not actually go into the market," she said, laughter in her eyes. "After the other day, Altiri'll take you to pieces."

"I can handle Altiri," he said, his dignity back in place.

He tugged at the brim of his hat. The sun was now at a level with the sea, and the sea was all aflame. "You can't be Miri's niece, really," he said.

Virginia had zipped up her jacket as she came down from the cottage porch. Now she pulled her hair free of the jacket collar and shook it out. They were walking back as he had come, along the cliff's rim, down to the stairs.

"I heard them talking about you at the hospital now and again, but I expected you to be a nice little old lady." He squinted into the sun. She laughed.

"*Grandniece.* I don't know if you knew this, but Miri sure thinks a lot of you," she told him, burying her hands in her pockets and looking out over the ocean. "She says you have one of the finest talents she's ever seen." Virginia glanced at him, and he thought he saw some respect in her face. He was embarrassed. "She's seen a lot of them, over the years," Virginia added. And there was that melancholy distance in her voice again.

"Miri's being kind when she talks like that," he said.

"Miri's never been kind that way," she corrected him. And then she fell silent. He was still embarrassed; he didn't want her thinking he was more than he was.

"Music is all I know," he said finally. "It doesn't make a life."

"No," she agreed. "You need more than one thing to make a life." She glanced at him again, tossing him a smile, changing the subject. "Sometimes when I look at you, I think I'm seeing Courtney."

They'd gotten to the head of the stairs. He couldn't look down them just now; therein lay great vertigo. He had to blink his eyes a few times to bring the horizon back to where it rationally should have been.

"Are you all right?" she asked.

"Yes." Not strictly the truth. "I just need to sit down for a moment. If you don't mind."

She didn't mind. She sat down in the grass at the side of the path, crossing her legs comfortably. There didn't seem to be any awkwardness or formality about her, nothing to make him feel anything but at home. He sat down beside her, thinking that he liked her very much, and he wanted her to like him.

"I was in an accident a couple of weeks ago . . ." Longer than that, actually. He wanted her to understand why he was a little slow.

"I know. They talked about it a lot."

"I had the nicest little black Jetta," he said wistfully. "Anyway, I got hurt. Here," he touched his temple, "and there were some complications. Nothing permanent—and things are beginning to get easier. It makes me impatient. Lately, everything makes me impatient." He pulled at a blade of the long, course grass, wishing he hadn't said the last thing. It was just that, with her, things had suddenly slowed down—all except his metabolism—and it was easy to talk. "Most of the time, I'm a little embarrassed," he admitted.

"Why?" she asked.

He looked into her face and saw that those windows were still open in her eyes. He looked back down at his hands; he didn't want to look into those eyes for very long because they muddled his thinking.

"I'm not usually this dizzy." He tossed the grass down over the edge of the hill. *Or this helpless,* he thought. *Or this stupid*—but then, he couldn't be so sure of that. "People keep asking me 'Are you all right?' I mean, it's nice that they should be concerned, but they've been asking so long now, I'm beginning to feel more like a little boy than a man all the time." He looked at her. "I *am* a man, by the way." He grinned.

"I noticed," she said and stood up. He was pleased. He stood up, too, taking one slow breath. She took his arm. "You ready?" she asked. He smiled to himself. It was a lovely little feminine gesture, this taking his arm; by it, she meant to keep him from falling headlong down those stairs, and he knew it. Still, he couldn't mind, not with her hand there on his arm, giving his nervous system a very pleasant case of the fits.

"Susan tells me you two used to play a lot of racquetball," she said. She was allowing him to take the stairs as he needed to, one at a time. Gone the little boy, enter the old man.

"I suppose she told you she always let me win," he said wryly.

"Nope," she said. The breeze blew tiny streamers of hair across her face when she turned to talk to him. "But she told me that's what she used to tell you."

He laughed. "That's what she used to tell me," he said. He was holding on to the railing with his free hand. "Did they tell you I used to play baseball?" he asked.

"No," she said.

He laughed again, this time for himself. "I'm glad there are a few things at least that Susan doesn't know about me. *I* used to play baseball."

"Susan's not that bad," Virginia said.

"Give her a while," he said.

"When did you play?" she asked.

He smiled. "It was pony league," he admitted. "So, it wasn't really *playing*, I guess. But I loved it. And I was pretty good at it, too." He pulled his hat down tight against the breeze and smiled at her from under the brim.

"But you quit?" she asked.

"Well, my mom didn't like me playing on Sundays. She was a good Catholic, and she had objections to that. *I* didn't care. I didn't have a religion then, except piano. I don't know; I could've been religious about baseball." He stopped on the halfway landing, putting his hand over hers. He closed his eyes momentarily.

She was very good about not saying anything. He opened his eyes, the dizziness past. "Okay," he said, his heart still pumping away heavily. He patted her hand gratefully.

"You weren't the shortstop, were you?" she asked.

"That's what I was," he said. "How did you know that?"

"That's what I played," she told him happily.

"Hey," he said. For the first time in a long time, he was having a good time.

"Where are you from?" she asked.

"Courtney's already told you," he said.

She opened her eyes wide. "That's right," she said.

"Anyway, you should be able to tell. Can't you hear the accent? Maybe I lost it."

"No," she said. "I hear it. But you just sound like everybody else in L.A. Did everybody in L.A. kind of immigrate here from New York?"

He laughed. "Just the ones with class," he said. There was one tiny seam of fire between the night sky and the dark ocean. He was glad they'd gotten to the bottom of the stairs before the light had disappeared completely. The thought of those stairs in the dark scared him now. He was awfully tired, and he was getting light-headed.

She got him talking as they crossed the sand. They went down to the edge of the water where the beach was firm and the walking easier. She asked him about school, and soon he was talking about things he'd practically forgotten that he'd forgotten—all those old feelings. Especially when they remembered the old songs from back then, he got the feelings.

He told her things he never would have thought to tell another human being, things about his old locker, and about girls, and about shooting toothpicks into the acoustical tile ceiling in the cafeteria.

She didn't say much, just asked a little question here and there. Once or twice he tried to ask her something about herself, but she sidestepped him so neatly that he never even noticed what she'd done, turning the conversation back to him. He wasn't really a talker, but she drew him out so completely and so easily. That was it—he was so entirely at ease with her, so absolutely comfortable. He even started to talk about his family, which he never had done with anybody but Courtney. He was turning himself quietly and completely inside out without even realizing it.

He knew he had pushed his body too hard by the time they reached Altiri's. His legs were aching, and his head was throbbing a little again. His stomach wasn't too pleased with him either, and the palms of his hands were chilling.

She still had her hand tucked in the crook of his arm. It had become such a familiar thing to him that he was disturbed when she took it away. "You don't really want to come in with me," she said.

"Right-o," he said. "I'll wait." And he stood there in the dark, watching as she passed easily through the bright cones of light that lit Altiri's parking lot. *That's a very nice lady,* he told himself. He turned away from the light and went down into the dark by the water, where he finally sat down.

He dug into the warm sand and hugged himself, closing his eyes and giving himself over to the noises of the evening. People were coming in and out of Altiri's. He could hear their voices faintly, the sound floating out into the dark, indistinguishable words, sometimes laughter. The cars went by on the Coast Highway, and the waves wove rhythm out of all of it—gentle, constant.

He must have fallen asleep. Somebody was patting his face softly and saying his name. He shook himself. "Oh, hello," he said thickly. She sat down close to him. He thought it would probably be very nice to kiss her.

"You're tired," she said.

"I'm tired," he agreed. He sighed. "Do you think you could carry me home?"

"I like you," she said, smiling. "Nobody's made me laugh for a long time."

"Was I funny?" he asked her.

"You want me to call Courtney?" she asked. Courtney and the old blue Volkswagen—he was beginning to hate the sight of it.

"No," he said.

"What do you want to do, then?" she asked.

Well, we could just sit here and kiss each other for a while, he thought cheerfully. He sighed again, and began to move around as if he meant to get up. She made it look as though they were helping each other up, but he suspected that she could have gotten herself up quite easily without anybody's assistance. She put her hand on his arm again, and he let her do it even though he would have preferred things otherwise; he wasn't sure enough of his balance to try walking in sand with his arm around anybody. They walked along the edge of the water silently for a time.

"Tomorrow night," Sidney said finally, "Courtney and Calvin—you know Calvin? Of course you do—and Susan and this friend of hers are going to be at my house for Trivial Pursuit, and they're going to play teams, and they're going to make me play by myself. Maybe you'd like to come? It's usually kind of fun. And I don't want to play by myself."

"We did that a couple of times while you were in the hospital," she said.

"At my house?" he asked, shocked. He was skewered with

jealousy. Here was this fine girl, in his house, and nobody even thought to tell him about it. "You'd think *Susan* would have said *something.*"

"You leave Susan alone," she said, pinching him lightly on the arm. That, too, was a satisfying thing, that she should feel comfortable enough with him to pinch him one. "She played cello in church a couple of weeks ago. It was really nice. Miri says the whole ward is going to think it's died and gone to heaven, getting Courtney and Susan both at the same time . . ."

"Wait a minute," he said, and he stopped walking because he was confused. "Getting them for what?"

"*Getting* them." She put her other hand up on his arm. "Don't tell me you didn't know?"

He stood there, letting himself be angry. It was one thing to be stupid and not see what was going on in his own house, but it was another having his friends sneaking around behind his back.

"It seems," he said stiffly, "there are things Susan *doesn't* talk about."

"I'm sorry," Virginia said. "I shouldn't have said anything."

"Why not? You're going to assume that lifelong friends should keep secrets from each other?" He made an exasperated sound and started walking again, glad of the energy the anger had given him. "Don't worry about it. *Susan* should be worried about it."

The lights of his house were just ahead of them. He stopped again and put a hand on her hand. "I'm not really mad," he said softly. "So don't worry about it, okay?"

"Okay," she said doubtfully.

"Just promise you'll come tomorrow night. Will you promise?"

She pulled down on his hat brim. "I'll come," she said.

"Meanwhile, if you don't mind, I think I'll have Calvin drive you home from here. Okay? That's a good girl." He was patting her hand absently, actually yearning after some kind of nice hug.

Twenty-one

There is nothing like the balmy, damp, spring sea air to pipe a person awake earlier than he might want to be in the morning. Sidney, particularly sensitive to such things today, woke, grabbing futilely at the lingering edge of a very nice dream, a _very_ nice dream, hoping to pull it back and wrap himself in it for just a few more blissful moments.

Not to be. The dream, with mincing step and mocking eyes, danced just out of his reach, until he opened his own eyes in vexation and became irrevocably awake.

Then he smiled. And then he sighed, because he remembered some of the dream. And the minute he remembered it, he knew he was going to have a hard time getting Virginia out of his mind. He didn't remember the details as much as the feeling—and, he realized with a gentle shock, some of the music. There had been a song in the dream, and he remembered it. He could hum it.

He sat up in the bed and hummed it to himself again. He wasn't going to be able to remember the chord structure, but he might be able to hit on it if he fiddled around on the keyboard long enough.

He pulled on his Levi's and padded out to the piano. Courtney was already in the kitchen, working away and singing to herself. He had to shut her voice out of his head entirely, grabbing hold of his own music with his whole brain so it wouldn't slip away again.

He struck a chord. The wrong chord. Almost a disaster—he caught the song by a few trailing threads and hummed it again, just to make sure.

"Hello," Courtney said. She was getting to be a fixture in his mind, standing just in the kitchen doorway that way. The house would be empty when she left. Now he smiled at her and waved, still humming, while he looked for the chord with his left hand.

"What's that?" she asked. He shook his head, still searching. She stood there for a moment more, then disappeared into the kitchen. He found the chord. He played it a couple of times so he wouldn't lose it again.

"Hello," he called, and then he started humming again.

"What do you want for breakfast?" she asked, coming to the door again. He held up one finger, and then he had the second chord. So far, so good.

"Steak and eggs?" he asked. "I don't mean to ignore you. I just . . ."

"You've got a song," she said. "I *did* live most of my life with you, you know. Steak and eggs? Aren't we getting ambitious?" She was grinning, and he knew it was because she felt that he must be getting his strength back. That was pleasure to her, and it made him feel nice and warm all over, knowing she cared about him like that. "Okay," she said, and retreated.

He found an intermediate chord that he liked very much. He ran the three chords, tracing out the melody with his right hand. *I might as well have one of those big, fat automatic mall organs*, he thought, impatient with his hands and his slow brain. "You guys could have told me about Virginia," he called. He heard her put the iron skillet on the stove.

"What?" she asked, sticking her face around the corner.

"You could have said something about Virginia," he said. He hit another chord, and then he changed it, and then he changed it again. None of them were right.

"Yes, we did," Courtney said. "Just a minute, I have to get the steak on." He ran the chords again, but they weren't working the way they should. "Argghhh," he said to himself.

Courtney came in and leaned against the big black piano, watching him. "We told you Miri's niece was here."

"Miri's niece," he said, trying a little figure with his right hand," would be about fifty. Virginia is her *grand*niece. There's a difference."

Courtney was watching his hands, grinning to herself. "A nice difference," she guessed. He glanced up at her, and he couldn't keep the grin off his own face. They could hear the steak beginning to sizzle and pop in the kitchen.

"And you never told me you'd had her over here," he said. He put his hands in his lap and looked at her.

"You needed to know that?" she asked.

"It would have been nice," he said, and he started playing again. She patted the piano once, smiling rather broadly now. The steak was begging for attention, and she went to see about it.

"So, tell me about her," he called as she went. He could hear her banging around in the kitchen, and she turned the steak.

"Didn't she tell you about herself?" Courtney called back. "Or," she said, peering at him from around the door frame, "were you too busy talking about yourself?"

"Oh, man," he said under his breath. "Just tell me. You'd think Susan would have said *something*."

"Susan's a little jealous of Virginia, I think. Envious, I mean."

"Why?" he asked, humming still, and making a mark on his paper.

"I don't know. You know Susan."

"So, *tell* me." A little bit of melody.

"She's Miri's niece," Courtney said, half-yell from the kitchen. "*Grand*niece, excuse me, and she comes out here every summer for a few weeks to visit, so you've probably met her before, and you don't remember. Or maybe you haven't." She peeked around the door again. "Have you?"

"For a few weeks?" he said with dismay.

She was opening the refrigerator now, still talking. "She's a psychologist, and she's a counselor at the University of Missouri. Ph.D. Impressive, huh?"

He had been in the middle of the chord progression, such as it was. Now he felt a kind of interior chill, and the little song was dead gone. Just like that. He put his hands in his lap and took a deep breath, and he just sat there.

He hadn't heard Courtney come in. She had her hand under his chin and was making him look at her. "Are you all right?" she asked. He wasn't all right. He'd spent the night dreaming about a psychologist. "Sidney?" Courtney's voice was a little scared. She was probably thinking it was the brain damage, finally showing up. He shook his head sharply, trying to shake off the sick feeling.

"I'm all right," he said. "But I think I'm going to go lie down."

"Okay," she said, only it came out more like a question.

"Why don't you take the steak off?" he said; he'd lost his appetite.

He went into his room and sat on his bed, and then he got up and went over by the window. It was beginning to cloud up out there over the ocean again. He thought he saw a flash of lightning over to the north. He went back to his bed and dropped himself on it, feeling terribly sorry for himself.

It was the most confusing feeling he'd ever had. He couldn't tell if he was angry or embarrassed or hurt or what. One thing, the better the up side felt, the worse the down side was going to be, and he had felt awfully good after that dream this morning.

Okay, now he could understand; they'd all been worried about him. For all he knew, he could have been severely depressed. So, all right—everybody's full of loving concern and along comes Miri's niece, who just happens to be smashingly charming and a psychologist to boot—it's the most natural thing in the world that she'd offer to check him out so his sister'd know if he was really crazy. And that explained how smooth she was, getting him to talk that way, just the right questions, a little probing into his childhood.

But the things he had *told* her. Private things. *Intimate* things. She'd made it so easy, as if she were really interested. He felt as though he'd taken off his clothes and run around naked in front of her. It would have been *fine* if they'd just *told* him. But no; instead, he's got to make an utter fool of himself, practically hugging somebody who was putting him through mental *examination*, for goodness' sake.

At least I didn't try to kiss her, he thought.

The worst thing was that the dream had been so nice. He put his hands behind his head and stared at the ceiling. *Yeah, well,* he thought, *you don't have a lot of luck with women, anyway. You fall in love with a Mormon, you fall in love with your nurse, you fall in love with your psychoanalyst. Don't you have anything better to do?*

By the time the evening came, he'd really dug himself into a hole. *They're all so* cute, he thought as Courtney got the game out and set it up. There wasn't one of them he couldn't have punched right in the nose. Susan and her little secrets and her big mouth. Cozy Calvin and Courtney.

It was a totally lousy evening. She walked into his house, and he might as well have been naked all over again, wondering what kind of conclusions she might have drawn. The bite was, she looked better to him then than she had the evening before. That, he didn't need.

It was depressing.

Sitting in the room with the finest girl he'd ever known, he felt like something you'd keep in a petri dish. He couldn't get into the spirit of the game; he couldn't get into the spirit of the conversation; he couldn't do anything but stare at the floor and sigh.

"You think *this* is fun, you ought to see him on one of his *good* days," Susan told Will. Sidney sympathized with Will—he seemed like such a pleasant person with his snapping black eyes and his good humor. *You'd have to have good humor to hang around with Susan,* Sidney decided.

It wasn't a terrific party. Finally Calvin left, taking Virginia with him, and Will was gone. Susan and Courtney were the only ones left, sitting there on the couch *looking* at each other.

"You're in a lousy mood, tonight," Susan said to him.

She shouldn't have said it. He stood up, burning a hole through her face with his eyes, and said, "You know, you could have said something about this whole church business. I may not be right on top of things, but I can understand the basics." He turned up the heat one notch. "I think you owed me that."

And then he went to bed.

He felt like death. He turned on his side and looked out of the window. A little later his door opened. "Sidney?" Courtney said. "You want to tell me what's going on?"

He didn't answer her.

"I know you're not asleep," she said. "You know, I used to think we knew each other pretty well, but I can't read you at all anymore. One minute you're up, then suddenly it's like the world comes to an end. So, okay, Susan made a mistake. *You've* made mistakes. Poor Virginia. You invite her here, and then you hardly say a word to her all night. Real nice, Sidney." She stopped for a moment. He stuck to his silence. "Sidney," she said quietly, "I know you when you're hurt. I'd think you could talk to me about it. Talk about owing people . . ." He heard the soft sound of the door closing, and the room was dark again.

He turned onto his back. Of course she was right.

But he didn't feel any better the next evening when he finally sat in front of Miri's piano for his lesson. He hadn't meant to be rude the night before, but what do you say to somebody who's busy x-raying your soul?

Of course, when he walked into Miri's parlor, *she* was there. It wasn't as though she had any reason to avoid him. She was sitting in her aunt's parlor, reading a book, and he couldn't help seeing how pretty she was, and he couldn't help feeling all upset inside, looking at her. As he stepped into the room, she'd looked up momentarily, the smile polite, so clinical and cool was she now. It was almost more than he could bear because the smell of her perfume had tinged the atmosphere of the room, and it was playing havoc with his nervous system. She was a grand-looking girl. Too bad for him.

"Take a breath and settle yourself," Miri said. She knew something was going on. Who wouldn't know? His hands were all shaky. *Someday, years from now, you won't remember anything about this feeling,* he told himself. *The nasty thing about being single is that your desire for any given girl is going to be directly proportionate to her aloofness.* This one he couldn't get out of his system to save his life.

"Are you going to play?" Miri was asking, looking at him quizzically.

He sighed, and he started the piece, the same old Bach that he could have played in his sleep. She stopped him, of course, and then he started over, and he didn't care if she stopped him a million times, because this wasn't what he wanted to be doing just now.

He was a few bars into it when there was a quick movement to the side of the piano. No one seemed to remark anything, so he kept on doggedly, butchering the music, but Miri never said a thing. He finished it eventually, nearly expecting a good hard rap across the knuckles for having played it so badly. But nothing happened, and he looked at his teacher.

Miri hadn't heard a note. She was sitting there, her face towards the door leading into the hallway, and she was lost in her own thoughts.

"I finished," he said.

She looked at him blankly. And then she pulled herself at least partly back into the present. "It was very good," she said absently. "Take these and go home and work on them." She tapped a small pile of music with her stick.

"That's it?" he asked.

"I'm tired," she said abruptly. "You go on home."

Now his feelings were hurt again. He stood there, waiting to help Miri up, but she evidently wasn't going anywhere, and she'd already forgotten him. So he picked up the music and left the room without another word. He showed himself to the door, and he closed it behind him feeling nothing but misery.

He stood on the porch for a moment in the bright moonlight. The air up here around Miri's garden always had such a heady, fine scent to it—sea-salt and roses, lilac and rain. He had turned towards the stair when a small noise caught him and stopped him where he was. He kept still, listening. It came again, the half-stifled sound of someone crying.

He put his music down on the chair and leaned against the railing for a moment, wondering what to do. He didn't want to intrude, but he hated to walk away from somebody who might need help.

"Hello?" he said softly. He didn't want to scare anybody.

There was a soft moan. Sidney climbed over the porch railing, stepping quietly onto the grass. "Do you need help?" he asked.

Then there was a strange, wet laugh. "Hi," the someone said reluctantly.

"Who is that?" he asked, following the sound of the voice to a dark, shallow cave under one of Miri's lilac bushes.

"It's me," she said, "It's Virginia." She sniffed.

"Are you all right?" he asked. She laughed again, better this time.

"Is it nice to be asking somebody else that for a change?" she asked. He sat on his heels and peered into the dark.

"What's wrong?" It never occurred to him that he should mind his own business.

"Oh . . ." she said, "I'm just remembering."

"You're not hurt?" he asked.

"That depends on what you mean," she said.

"Do you want me to leave you alone?" It was creeping back in now, the awareness of self. He was hoping she might need him to stay.

"I'm all right," she said. He was deeply disappointed. "Unless you *want* to stay," she added. Disappointment deferred. "There's room in here," she offered, and he could hear her moving over. For a moment he wondered if this was such a wise thing for him to do. But then wisdom is only one aspect of expediency. He got down on his knees and crawled into the dark, suddenly very pleased—in a concerned sort of way.

He fit himself in beside her, the lilacs soft and fragrant all around. She was still sniffing a bit. "What were you remembering?" he asked. He asked it very gently, making it so that she wouldn't have to answer if she didn't want to.

"My mother," she said, and her voice caught. He put his arm around her. She leaned her head on him, and she went on, her voice soft and sad. "She used to play that same Bach piece you were playing. At night, after I'd go to bed—the piano was downstairs right under my room—she'd play that. It was like home to me. It always meant she was there, even though she'd left me in the dark."

He patted her arm. It was clear her mother didn't do that anymore.

He put his head back against the house.

"You know," she said after a while, "the irony of it is, I used to counsel people all the time about grief. I used to know a *lot* about that."

Sidney could remember giving that kind of counsel himself

once or twice in the last few years, and now, sitting here in the dark with the reality fresh and sore beside him, he thought he must have been darned cheeky to do it.

She sighed. "I came out here to California because I thought I could deal with it here, with Miri here. There's really nothing for me at home anymore. Just my job. My dad died a long time ago, and my brothers and sisters are all over the country with their own families." He wished he had a handkerchief to offer.

When she spoke again, her voice was low and quiet. "At first, I was scared because I couldn't *cry*. But you sure helped."

He sighed and rested his cheek against her head. He was tired again.

"And it was nice walking with you the other night," she said. "It was nice to have something else to think about for a while."

He smiled grimly to himself. "I talked too much," he said.

"No," she whispered. "Just what the doctor ordered."

"You know," he said, "Miri's in there worrying about you. Maybe you'd better cry inside." He gave her a sharp little hug with the one arm. "Don't you think? You need to cry alone?"

She laughed. "I like it here," she said. "At least, it's warmer now that you're here." Not unpleasantly warm, either. "It's so strange," she said, "that I should feel so lost, but I went out into the dark for comfort." Her voice was getting clearer. "The more I know about myself, the less I know about people. You know, Sidney, it strikes me that life is a very thin thing."

He thought about Miri and Courtney and Calvin and Susan, how *present* and permanent they were to him, but how easily they could be broken and gone—in a second's time, in the breath of a moment—history, a memory, gone along with the rest of the things the years lay to rest. He was glad of the house at his back. He was glad of the girl, warm and alive, beside him.

He put his cheek down on her head again, not a romantic gesture, but a human one. And he thought, *Okay. So maybe she was doing Courtney a favor. So maybe she was giving me a good, clinical going over. Okay. She's got her own problems, and she's a nice person, and she needs somebody to take care of her. Not somebody to consume her—take care of her. You could do that. You could stop being an adolescent jerk and start acting like an adult Christian, and make sure this girl gets taken care of, can't you?*

I believe, Sidney my man, you can do that. You just be her big brother, and you can forget the damp palms and the whole thing. Only, maybe you'd better ask her not to wear that perfume anymore, because it's going to be very hard to be objective when you can smell that.

"Come on," he said, giving her a little push. *You just remember, he told himself, you just think of yourself as a big brother, and help her through this time, and she can get on with her life.* "I'm not going to leave you out here, and I've got to go home."

He crawled out of the lilacs, then he pulled her out after.

"Thanks," she said, suddenly a little awkward and shy.

Then he remembered last evening, and he was ashamed of himself. "I'm sorry about last night," he said. "I don't think I'm very rational sometimes."

She laughed. "It's okay," she said. "I was afraid you were mad at me."

He couldn't think of anything to say to that, so he pointed at the front door. "In," he said. "I'm going to stand here until you go."

She folded her arms and went obediently. She stopped at the top of the stairs. "Good night," she said. Then she was gone.

He was halfway home before he realized he'd left Miri's music on the porch. He had to creep back and get it. When he could see the light of his own house again, he was happy. His life was going on in there, and he was glad to be able to climb into it again.

An hour later Sidney was sitting in his chair, lulled by the quiet flow of talk. There were deep shadows in the corners of the room, and he was drowsy, but he still wanted to hear them talk, his sister and his friends. It was a happy, safe sound, whatever it was they were talking about.

He sat with the tips of his forefingers against his lips, staring into the air. "You want some lemonade?" Susan asked. He smiled from behind his fingers. "No, thank you," he said. She was still looking at him, and then he remembered what he'd said to her the night before. He put out his hand and he took hers, holding it momentarily. She smiled at him, and he felt terrible because her face was so transparent, asking if he really meant it was okay.

"It's okay," he said. "I'm sorry I'm such a dog."

"I have to say I'm glad Miri gave you something new to work on," Courtney said from across the room. She had the music in her hands. "Brahms. At least it'll be a change."

Calvin and Will were having a very sober discussion relative to the state of the American farmer. The women settled down together, having lost themselves in an argument over some Nietzschean philosophy. Sidney closed his eyes and drifted, more at peace in this single moment than he'd been for years, perhaps because just now he knew what he had, and he knew what it meant. He almost didn't care about music anymore. This feeling of peace was filling in whatever place in him had been vacant; and he knew, if it came down to that, he could learn to sell shoes. Anyway, he'd given it to God; it wasn't his problem anymore.

Long after he'd taken himself to bed, the discussions went on, and woven through it all, the tides—constant, independent of all the intentions of any man—also in the hands of God.

Twenty-two

It had been a long time since Sidney had passed so pleasant a night.

And when he began to wake early the next day the room was full of music. He lay very quietly, his eyes half-open, keeping very still. It was as if there were bright, magic beings here, and he wouldn't have frightened them away for the world. But run they finally did, one by one, gone away until the room was empty and silent, and he was awake once more, remembering every note of it, every tiny movement.

He sat up happily, and he still remembered.

Now, if only Courtney weren't up yet, he could make _her_ some breakfast. He pulled on a sweat shirt and his jeans, and he got to work.

"You want to tell me what you're doing?" Courtney asked. She was standing there in the kitchen doorway, holding on to her robe, comfortably tangled and frowzy.

"Making breakfast," he said.

"At six?" she asked, trying to run her fingers through her hair.

"How late were you up?" he reproved, putting his hands on his hips just the way she would have done.

"Never mind," she said. "What are you making?"

"Steak," he announced, slapping the freezer door shut, "and eggs."

"Hmmm," she said.

"So if you're going to take a shower, do it. You wouldn't want to waste perfectly good hot steak and eggs."

"I certainly wouldn't want to do that," she murmured, shuffling away. He put the steaks on, and then he leaned against the sink. Chris was back in town now. They were scheduled to go into the studio very soon—at the end of next week, in fact. He couldn't help the nerves. It wasn't going to be an easy experience, going in there without any tools, the way he was going to have to.

He pushed himself away from the sink. *You'll just have to do it*, he told himself. *Meanwhile, you've got plenty to keep you busy.*

Two little sisters—the real one and the adopted one—that was enough to keep anybody busy. He'd lost some time with the real one, and now she really didn't need him all that much anymore. He didn't intend to waste time with the adopted one. The trick was going to be giving care without hovering, being buddies without crowding her.

So on that Saturday evening, when Courtney and Susan were baptized at last, he made sure that Virginia felt a part of things. And he made himself useful the next day, making sure she had somebody to talk to, being careful not to dominate her attention. He made her laugh as often as he could. That wasn't easy; he wasn't a terrifically funny person. But he was doing his best. And he was staying out of her way. Some dashing professional type (who looked to Sidney more like a surfer in a suit) caught sight of her just before the first meeting started, and he came up and introduced himself—new in the area, didn't know anybody, didn't know where anything was, where did she go to school?

Sidney folded his arms and stood aside, listening to the man talk. He even suffered it silently when the man followed them all into the meeting, still talking, and sat down next to Virginia, taking the last seat in the pew so Sidney had to sit behind.

Now, he reasoned with himself, *if I were her* real *brother—which I can't help once in a while remembering I'm not—I wouldn't let her go out with this guy. He's pompous, he's shallow, he's aggressive, and he probably drives a nice car.*

Sidney's opinion hadn't changed materially by the time Sunday School was half over and the guy finally got around to asking her out. *Has he even spoken a word to me?* Sidney asked himself. *Has he so much as acknowledged the fact that I'm here?* The thought that Sidney could have gone off on his own, leaving her in good enough hands, never entered his head. And when this person asked her out, he invited her to a *rock* concert, no less. And then she told him she'd go.

Steady on, old man, Sidney told himself, grabbing his primeval desires by the scruff of the neck and reminding himself of his self-determined function in this girl's life. *He seems like a nice enough young man, doesn't he? So he probably drives a nice car and goes to board meetings; it's not like he's going to do her any harm. Which I'll kill him for if he does.*

Then Courtney invited everyone over for dinner—the regulars and Virginia and Miri (*not,* mercifully, the surfer, although he wouldn't have put it past her). Miri declined very gracefully, and Virginia demured for Miri's sake. As it happened, Miri didn't *want* anybody demuring for her, and Virginia was more or less ordered to go down with the other young people and have a good time. And that was what she did.

It might have been an echoing of an antiquity, the men all together in the half-light of the main room, full of dinner, speaking together in contented and drowsy tones about the State of Things in General, while the women continued their labors in the kitchen, a bright counterpoint of laughter and light. And these particular men *might* have felt a kinship with the Earthly Lords of Other Times, if they had not just been almost bodily thrown from that same kitchen only moments before, protesting all the way that they really, sincerely *liked* doing dishes.

It was a sweet and heady evening. The windows had been thrown open to the wild and warm open air, breezes stirring gently in the corners of the room, lifting the corner of a page here, the leaf of a plant there. Alistair's wisteria had gotten into the air, and the whole room was a bower of briny spring serenity.

Eventually, the light in the kitchen went off, and the women came in to join their talk to the men's. Susan sat next to Will on the couch, Courtney found a place on the arm of Calvin's chair, and Virginia chose the floor near Sidney, much to his pleasure.

And the evening wagged on into night. Will's voice was deep and rich like Susan's cello, mellow as the wisteria; Sidney nearly fell asleep, listening to it. And then Virginia had to leave. "I have work tomorrow," she had to explain. This was news to Sidney. "I'm counseling at the UCLA Institute three days a week," she told him. Calvin stood up, sighing. They hadn't even had the pie yet.

Sidney, from deep in his chair, raised one hand and said, "I'll take care of her." And then to her, "You don't mind walking?"

"I don't mind," she said, and he rose from his chair.

"You'll be coming for family home evening tomorrow?" Calvin asked, looking first at Virginia and then at Will.

"Y'all are the *strangest* people," Will sighed.

"But you will come?" Calvin pursued.

"I'll ask Miri," Virginia promised. Susan poked Will until he succumbed to the pressure and promised to attend.

"Evening, all," Sidney said, holding out a jacket he'd found for Virginia. He opened the front door for her and ushered her into the night.

"Did you have a good day?" he asked easily, the light of his house behind them and the fine starry sky above. She put her hand on his arm again. He covered it with his own.

"It was a wonderful day," she said. And then she fell silent.

"I think," he said, "you should make me talk some more." He was wondering if she was still supposed to be figuring him out.

"You're not really a talker, are you?" she observed.

"Not when I can listen," he said.

She laughed. "You don't want to talk now," she said.

"Yes, I do. There's a lot I didn't tell you. There may be things Susan hasn't told you yet, you never know. All I need is the questions."

"All right," she said slowly, putting her hand on the hand he had over her hand. "Tell me about how you decided to join the Church."

That was an easy question. He told her the whole story, everything including smatterings of childhood religions, leaving out only Emily's name because Emily as Emily didn't seem relevant anymore. It turned out to be a good long story, what with the mission thrown in. It got them all the way up the stairs to the cliff's edge.

"Do you mind if we sit down?" she asked. What a grand little faker she was. Here he was, breathing like a horse, and she—breathing like an angel—wanted to sit down.

"I don't mind at all," he said. They found a place in the grass away from the path a little, right on the edge where they could look out over half the world. She wrapped her arms around her knees and asked him, "What do you love most in the world? Besides specific people, I mean."

"Music," he said.

"Miri says you're gifted," she said.

"I have been," he said. She looked at him quizzically. "Well," he said reluctantly, "it's kind of a long story."

He told her, of course. And this, too, was a very long story. He started in the middle and then he had to go back, and then he had to go back further, and she listened, asking a quiet question here and there until she had the whole thing, or everything he knew how to put into words. *There,* he thought, *analyze* that.

She stared pensively into the night sky for a long time after he'd finished. "You know," she said, "it's kind of like that for me, too. I mean, I don't hear music. Well, I do—I hear it, but I don't hear it like you do. What I mean is, *I* have a gift, too, kind of. That's why I finally went into counseling. It's like, I *feel* things beyond what people have said. Does that make sense? People talk, and I can feel what they mean, almost the way you'd feel different textures. Does that sound weird? And like you, the only thing I can feel these days is my own feeling." She put her chin on her knees. "Except when you talk," she added, and he could see that white smile through the dark.

"Would you mind very much," she said, "calling me Ginny? It's kind of a special name to me." She was getting sad on him again.

"If *you* don't mind," he said, not sure he was comfortable with the honor.

"I'd like it," she said, and she stood up. He stood up too, not without a good deal of reluctance. She took his arm, and they walked toward Miri's. "What did you think of Peter this morning?" she asked.

"Peter?" he said.

"The one who sat beside us in Sunday School."

"Oh," Sidney said, trying hard to keep any stray abrasiveness out of his voice. "He was nice," he said, as neutrally as possible, all things considered.

"Very *nice* looking, didn't you think?" she asked. He could have sworn there was laughter in the words.

"For a Californian," he allowed. "But, you know, it's hard for me to judge, being basically the same sex. What did you think?"

"He was nice," she said. And she *was* laughing, and he didn't see what was so funny.

And there was Miri's cottage, all too soon, bright amber windows like the home beacon beaming. Sidney sighed.

Virginia-now-Ginny turned to him and gave him a swift kiss on the cheek. "You're very good to me," she said. "Don't think I don't appreciate it. I haven't had a friend like you in a long time."

He was totally chagrined.

"I'll see you tomorrow night," she said. She left him for the house and was received at last into a golden rectangle of light. He watched long after the door had closed, hoping she'd realize she still had his jacket, hoping she'd have to come back out again and bring it to him. He had to give it up at last because there was a cool wind beginning to come in off the sea, and he was beginning to shiver.

Virginia knocked on Miri's open door, peeking around the edge of it. Miri sat in her bed holding a book, hair in paper curls, cheeks rosy pale, smiling at her grandniece. She put her book down and patted the edge of the bed, inviting Virginia to sit.

"You've had a good time," Miri observed.

Ginny wondered where, exactly, it showed. "Yes," she said. "I did. You should have come," she added, pinching at her aunt's quilt-draped leg.

"Oh, no," Miri said. "There's a season to everything. This —" she held up the book, "is mine, now. Who brought you home?" she asked, getting right down to the truth of the matter.

"Sidney did," Ginny said, facing her aunt down.

"He's a nice boy," Miri said. She'd said it easily a hundred times in the last few weeks.

"He's been very nice to me," Ginny said.

"You like him," Miri said.

"I think we're going to be friends," Ginny said, begging the question.

"But you do *like* him," Miri said.

"Wasn't that the way you wanted it?" Ginny asked, grinning.

"Cheeky girl," Miri said affectionately, but she didn't return the grin. "Oh, I just hope . . . ," she said thoughtfully.

"What?" Ginny asked.

"Has he ever told you about Emily?" Miri asked.

"No," Virginia said, suddenly and unaccountably uneasy.

Miri sighed. "I don't know what that means," she said to herself. "Do you think he likes you?" she asked.

"I don't know," Virginia said, suddenly realizing that she really didn't know, and, more than that, understanding how much she had been enjoying the assumption that he did.

"Well, you go on to bed and don't worry about it. It was just Susan talking. I'm sure he'll tell you about it if it's worth telling. Which it probably isn't and I shouldn't have said anything. Now you go off to bed." She shooed Virginia off the bed and out of the room into the dark hall.

Virginia turned on the light in her own room, and then turned it off again. She went to the window and stood there, looking out into the dark, empty sky. She wanted to know about Emily, whatever she was. She *had* to know about Emily. There was more involved here than she had realized, and she wasn't sure how much she could afford to invest.

Twenty-three

"I don't know. She just said she wasn't going to come." Courtney, out on the front porch, was brushing the sand off her legs. She leaned against the door with one hand, lifting each leg in turn as she brushed. She had shorts on and a tee shirt, and she had her hair pinned up behind her head. "And she said she probably wouldn't make it Thursday either." She slipped her sandals back on and pulled her towel off the porch rail.

He leaned back against the bookcase and folded his arms, frowning.

"Would you get me my Hansen's out of the fridge, please?" his sister asked.

"Maybe I'd better call her," he said. "I wonder if she's sick or something?" He went into the kitchen.

"You can't call her; she's at work, and anyway, it's probably no big thing," Courtney said. "It's probably Miri," she called after him. "She doesn't like to leave her. Anyway Virginia didn't sound sick."

He came back out of the kitchen and handed her a can.

"This was in the fridge?" she asked.

He looked at the can blankly for a moment. "I guess . . . No." He took it out of her hand. It was quite warm. He made an exasperated sound and headed back into the kitchen. "I'm sorry," he said.

When he came back, she was grinning at him. "I think it's cute that you're so concerned about her. You've really got it bad this time, don't you?"

"Do you *mind*?" he said, and he went back inside to lean against the bookcases. "There just happens to be a very nice, simple *relationship* developing here."

"I *see*," she said.

"And Virginia has no more than a clinical interest in me, anyway, as you well know."

"What do you mean, as I well know?"

He pushed himself upright. "I have work to do," he said. He sat down at the piano and began to play.

Courtney sat down in the doorway, watching. "What're you playing?" she asked. "It's very nice." She buffed at her hair with the towel, and then she turned away from the door and pulled the top off the Hansen's.

"This is one of Chris's songs for the album. I think I've just about got it here. The chord chart, anyway," he said.

"When's C.J. coming? Why don't you come out here and sit with me for a while?"

"No, thanks," he said. "It's too hot for hats, and I don't want to get sunburned. He's going to be here in a few minutes anyway, and I'm not ready for him yet."

He picked up his pencil and tapped the paper thoughtfully before he made a few marks on it. The tune was still stiff and he knew it, but things were getting better. Last night he'd heard some beautiful things, and he'd found them on the piano this morning. There was that one song he'd heard the other night, the one in his dream about Ginny. He'd heard it again last night, and he knew he was going to get it down, sooner or later.

Then C.J. came, and things really got cooking. They went through the song, working on the chords and throwing around some ideas about percussion, and then they went on to one of Graham's tunes. At five o'clock they quit. They had to quit by five because C.J. said Kinsey would kill him if he got home late on a nonsession day.

"I think it's going to work," C.J. said, rubbing down the neck of his guitar with the old red bandanna he always kept in the case. "You're warming up," he went on. "This stuff is pretty good."

"Thanks," Sidney said. "Let's hope Graham thinks so." He erased some stray marks off the score sheet.

"He didn't dislike the last stuff," C.J. told him.

"He was being nice. There wasn't a lot about it to like," Sidney said. "And I think I remember that he gave me a big lecture about something." He couldn't remember much about it, except that it hadn't been one of his better moments. "By the way, Graham said you'd been doing a little lecturing of your own."

C.J. put his instrument away with infinite care. "About what?" he asked. He closed the lid and started snapping down the latches.

"Doctrinal stuff," Sidney said. He folded the manuscript paper closed.

C.J. grinned at him. "Oh, yeah." He set the case on end and sat down in one of the chairs. "We've been talking about that a lot. Graham's pretty interested in that kind of thing these days. And Nancy and the kids are right there, know what I mean? She's really into it. It's a nice feeling, teaching people who listen."

"So you've been proselyting, eh?"

"I didn't get to go on a mission," C.J. reminded him.

"Didn't *get* to?" Sidney repeated.

"Well, however you want to put it. But I'm not doing too badly with Graham and his family. It was a very natural thing, actually. You laid all the ground work, anyway."

"*I* did," Sidney said.

"Oh, yeah," C.J. said, standing and picking up his case. "He was pretty impressed when you threw everything over to go on your mission. He really thought that was something fine."

"I didn't do it to impress anybody," Sidney said. C.J. looked at him like maybe he hadn't heard him right.

"Yes you did," he said.

"Who?" he asked, and then he remembered. "Yeah, I guess I did," he said. Emily, of course.

"How come you haven't called her for the last three weeks, man?" C.J. asked.

"What difference does it make?" Sidney asked.

"What do you mean, what difference does it make? She's been sitting around making up excuses for you. Look, I think I'd better explain something to you. Why do you think she came here this summer? You think a girl like that would be a *reception-ist* at Cap's when she could be interning at some big Japanese corporation? She stayed here because of you. And she's been sitting around, waiting for you to call her."

"Oh," Sidney said. "Look, I never—"

"I know it." C.J. cut him off. "I told her. I don't know what she expects after the way she treated you. It's not your fault."

"How was *I* supposed to know it mattered to her one way or the other?" Sidney asked him. "And she's waiting around for me to call her?"

"It's kind of pathetic," C.J. said. "I knew this was going to happen."

"It just wasn't worth it anymore." Then why was he feeling so guilty?

"I know," C.J. said. "But *she* doesn't know, and somebody's going to have to tell her. And *I'm* not going to do it."

"Kinsey?" Sidney asked, hopefully.

"Are you kidding?" C.J. asked. "Anyway, she's not going to take it from anybody but you. Of course, you could just let things go, and after a year or two she'd get the idea. She thinks you're still on your death bed, by the way. She keeps asking me how we're going to record on Saturday when you're still all wiped out."

Sidney closed his eyes. "Okay," he said. "Just do me a favor and don't let her show up at that Saturday session, okay? Tell her it's not a good idea. And then, maybe the next week . . ."

"Not Saturday," C.J. said.

"Do *not* let her come," Sidney said. "I've got plans."

C.J. nodded. "Poor Emily," he said.

"Poor Sidney," Sidney said, and C.J. had to agree.

All evening Sidney missed Ginny. It wasn't because every-body else *had* somebody, or because they made him play on a team all by himself. It was not for any definable reason, really. He just missed her. And he worried about her. He knew she was in good hands with Miri, and he knew Miri was probably better off with somebody to look after, but knowing those things only took the edge off his own feeling that something very sweet was missing.

He wished he could have talked to her some time, just a word or two after she'd gotten home from work. But no one had answered the phone at Miri's all evening, and he put himself to bed early.

He had a troubled night, his sleep interrupted by noises he couldn't wake up enough to identify. When he could finally get his eyes open to listen, it was the presun dawn, still dark in the room, and the room—he was shocked to realize—was drowned in music. Great, crashing, turbulent music, wall-to-wall, welling up in his ears and deafening him to anything else. Beethoven. The *Eroica.*

He sat straight up in bed. It was so loud and so wild, this music, that he wondered if someone were out in the living room, playing it on the piano. But no, there were full strings in this, and horns and woodwinds and *tympani.* He glanced at the door, afraid the noise was going to wake up Courtney.

He put his hands over his ears. And then he brought them, the two hands, slowly around to where he could see them. He stared at them for a long time, and then he lowered them to his knees. He began to move his fingers, and then suddenly the music was running through him like a live current.

He threw the covers off and bounded across the room, barely remembering to pull on his pants. And then he was sitting in front of the piano. He sat still for a moment, rubbing his fist across his chin. Then he put his fingers down on the keyboard. The current was still there, and the keyboard began to yield up the music. It was a magnificant slash of color across the dark silence of the house, a fountain of clear sound, an incredible emotional outburst.

"What are you *doing?*" Courtney asked, standing there in her robe, staring at him out of the tangle in her dark hair.

"I'm playing," he said, and he slipped into the Bach, rendering it magnificently, and with all his comfortable old trashy technique.

"It's not even *six,*" she said.

He launched himself into Ravel, and then went off into Offenbach, coming back round to Beethoven. He beamed at her and played a little blues riff at the end.

"You're really *playing*," she said.

"Isn't it great?" he asked. Another blues figure came down. He got up and came around the piano and hugged her. Then he let her go and did a funny little dance into the kitchen, singing "We're going to have pancakes, pancakes . . ." as he opened the refrigerator door.

But Courtney was still standing beside the piano, watching him. "Sidney," she said, a warning in her voice. He stood there with the milk and eggs in his hands, all innocence.

"I don't want to spoil this for you," she said, "but . . . ," she sighed, "I think maybe you'll want to know. I talked to Miri last night. Virginia thinks she'd better not come down here anymore. And she specifically mentioned you. She doesn't want to see you. Did you make a pass at her the other night?"

"No!" he said indignantly. He put the milk and the eggs down on the table.

"And what was that big crack you made yesterday about how I should know—what did you say—like "something" she was interested in you?"

"Clinically," he said.

"What was that all about?"

"You know," he said.

"I do *not*," she said. "But I would love for you to tell me."

He began to have doubts. And things were getting awkward. He went around behind the table and thoughtfully opened the milk.

"You drink that out of the carton again, and you're dead meat," she said. "Now, you'd better tell me what you're talking about, Horatio."

"I just thought . . ." he said, thinking it sounded a little irrational, now that he had to say it, "maybe . . . you, being worried about me, and Virginia being a psychiatrist . . ."

"*Psychologist*. And you thought . . . You *didn't*."

"Well . . ." he said.

"I can't believe how egocentric you've gotten," she announced. "The whole world does *not* revolve around you, Sidney," she said. "People do not base their whole lives and relationships with other people on *you*. I'm going back to bed. I think you truly are out of your mind." She turned on her heel and went to her room.

"So you didn't put her on me?" he called after her. "Nobody did?" Things were beginning to look up. Courtney slammed her door. "Get lost," he heard her yell.

It seemed like a good idea. He grabbed his hat and his jacket, and he left the house. He stood on the porch and took a deep breath. *This is a healthy man,* he told himself, and there were little sparks of music going off around him. It was going to be a fine day, a fine day—just the right mix of summer and spring. There were gulls crying and the inland birds were making a tremendous noise. There was something in the air that put fire in his blood and filled his chest up with something that very badly wanted to *breathe.*

So he headed up the cliff stairs, all the way thinking in Mozart. When he got near the top, he could see the light caught in the grass on the edge above him, tiny shards of brilliance studded all along the round and dewy line that separated earth from sky.

He sat down on the top step, resting, and he looked out on the sleepy world. The Mozart went away. He sat there watching the sun-silvered gulls hanging in the air against the still, dark sky over the ocean, and he began to hear a gentle Palestrina, unhurried, the soul of another man's vernal-wrung heart caught in it, ancient and familiar as his own feeling, full of the sweet and poignant promises of youth.

Courage, old man, he told himself. *There is not a woman in the world who says she does not want to see someone she couldn't care less about seeing.* He stood up and went his way, whistling. Whatever had happened Sunday night, whatever had set Ginny off, it must have been a misunderstanding. It must have been, right? Because he hadn't stepped out of line at all. Not for a minute.

He began to be a little uneasy in his mind.

And then he could see the cottage. He saw the planters on the porch, and he could see into the yard. He was wondering which of the windows in that house was hers, when he saw somebody kneeling by the flower bed in the back, the one right along the cliff edge.

Oh, wow, he thought. *If that's her, I'm not ready, and I don't want her turning around and seeing me here before I know what I'm doing.*

He stopped, undecided. He wasn't sure he wanted her to know he'd come up here because of her, because what if he'd been right in the first place, and she thought he was nice, but nothing remarkable? Or what if she really meant it when she'd called him 'friend'? It wasn't as though he wanted to make a total fool of himself, going on egocentric (thank you, Courtney) assumptions. What was he going to say if she saw him? "Oh, hi, I just decided to come up here for a casual walk, where the only thing I could possibly run into is your yard, thanks. How are you?"

Okay, he either had to go ahead like an idiot, or turn around and run like an idiot. Of course, that person by the flowers *could* be Miri, pulling weeds the way she always did in the morning. And that was a very rational thought. *Fear does that to you,* he thought, *makes you irrational. You get scared of nothing.*

You can say hello to Miri. Who could find fault? She gives you Brahms. You have to at least stop and say "thanks for the triplets."

So fine. So he went on. But then, of course, it did turn out to be Ginny, on her knees in the grass, wearing some Greek-looking dress that had no business being on somebody weeding a garden in the wet grass. As he walked on, he saw that she was no longer working with the flowers but, having folded her hands into her lap, was gazing out at the ocean. Then she turned and saw him, and if anything in the world had ever been too late, this was it.

He waved. It was a totally nerdish thing to do, as if he were washing a window or something. He wanted to kick himself. And then *she turned away,* just as though she hadn't seen him. He stood there wondering if people could actually die of embarrassment.

He stopped dead.

He would have turned around and gone home, but how could he do that? It would be like having somebody fly over in a plane with one of those banners attached: This Jerk Thinks He's in Love with You.

But now she was standing up and coming this way. Okay, she wasn't looking at him, but she *was* coming this way. But then, how else was she going to get into the house without coming in this general direction? *Oh, but wait. We have a girl looking up, here, and* waving, *albeit reluctantly.*

His face was hot, and the insides of his ears were hot, and he could feel his pulse there, and he really wished he'd gone out for breakfast or something before he'd taken this on. He smiled at her. And he kept right on walking.

There was a little gate into the back yard that had a rose trellis over it. The gate was closed. That's where he stopped. She stopped on her side. She smiled at him. He nodded.

"Hi," he said.

"Hi," she said.

"You're up early." He was thinking, *That's right; let's get totally suave.*

The pearly opalescence of the morning was giving way to just daylight.

"So are you," she pointed out.

And this is really a stimulating discussion we've got going here, he thought. He said, "You always get up this early?" There was this little song running through his brain: "shut upshutup-shutup."

"No," she said. She shook her head a little and a strand of hair fell into her face. She brushed it aside, and as he watched her hand, his own hand moved a little. "Just when I'm here." She turned her face away again so that she could look out into the sky. There was a gull sort of hovering, almost even with the edge of the cliff. Sidney had a sudden impression of the space under the gull, and it made him feel funny.

"When I was little," she said, her voice tight, "when I used to come out here and stay with Aunt Miri, I was always up early, before anybody else, and I used to sit near the edge of the cliff—

well, not very near—and I'd sit there and look down at all those little houses down there along the beach and watch the people wake up. I always wondered what the people were like who could live in houses like those. Right on the beach, that way." She turned and gave him another one of those little, sad smiles. The inside of his chest went all sort of runny.

"Now you know," he said, scintillating to the last. He found himself wishing she'd stop listening to herself so much and *hear* him.

Still smiling she looked down at the grass. Then she slipped her hand up under one of the slats in the trellis and looked at him.

"You never told me about Emily," she said.

Oh dear, he thought, and then he mentally cursed Susan for the hundredth time. "Ummm . . . ," he said, "I didn't think of it."

She turned her face away again, a profile. It was nice. The line of her jaw was a little tight, maybe, but all in all, it was a very nice profile. He sighed.

"There's really not that much to tell," he said. And then he was inspired. "Why do you want to know?"

More profile—tighter jaw this time. A little shine at the eye. Then she shrugged. "I'm getting too old for this," she said. It came out like a capitulation. "I'll tell you why. Because I don't want to get involved with a man who's already involved with somebody else. That's why. And I don't think I can be *with* you and not get involved. Now, is that honest enough for you?" She averted her face again. "I don't think I can stand—" catch in the throat "—any more emotional stress right now." She was sniffing again. "I really like you," she added. It sounded so hopeless the way she said it. She was walking all over her pride to get it out, and you had to admire her for that.

He didn't want to grin. More than anything else in the world he did not want to grin at that moment. But it was coming on anyway. There was a magnificent welling up in his bosom of all sorts of delightful things, and his face was not going to sit there and pretend that nothing was going on. So he looked down. But it wasn't enough. She saw it. He saw her see it—just peripherally, just in time to get a hand on her wrist before she could take off on him.

"Don't go," he begged. "I'll tell you anything you want to know. Only don't go."

She leaned back against the trellis and looked at him. He let her go. A delicate music came into him then, transparent as air.

"Should I make you tell me about the men you left behind?" he asked. "Or maybe you should tell me what's so great about Peter?"

There was the tiniest smile in her face. *Yeah*, he thought, *what is so great about Peter?*

"Susan thinks you're still in love with Emily," Ginny said.

"Susan can . . . ," he said, thinking of a number of different ways he could have ended the statement.

"Well, so, you're not. And I have . . . ," she said, looking down, "made a fool of myself for no good reason." She smiled at him apologetically.

"I'm glad you did," he said. "See, you saved *me* from having to do it. Because I came up here to tell you . . ." He felt his cheeks going red, and he kept grinning when he didn't want to, so he couldn't look her straight in the face. "I loved you the minute I saw you."

She laughed. "You were sick then," she said.

He was injured. "That was a matter of *balance*, not judgment. Anyway. You seem to be kind of interested in Peter." He was beginning to feel sorry for himself again.

"He did ask me out," she pointed out. "Nobody else around here has done that."

"Well, hey—" he said, "how about Friday night?"

"That's Peter's night—" she started.

"Don't go out with him, Ginny," he pleaded. "Come with me instead, and I'll make it up to you. I'll take you to the session on Saturday. I mean, I think you might find it interesting. I mean, it's a real recording session. If you're interested in that kind of thing."

Now she was grinning, and she wasn't looking at him either. "You want me to break my date," she said.

"Well, to tell you the truth, I was kind of hoping you'd come help me buy a car today."

"Sidney," she said. "So you want me to come with you today and then Friday night and Saturday? You don't waste any time."

"Not when it's important," he said.

"Do you give everybody this line?" she asked.

"Not usually," he said. He was trying to tone the grinning down, but he could tell it was coming out of his eyes and there wasn't a thing he could do about it.

"I can't go with you today," she said. It was as if she'd just thought of something, and she wasn't happy about it. "What time is it?"

He looked at his watch. "Almost seven."

"Oh no! I've got to be at work in an hour."

"Do you have to go?" he asked, unable to bear the thought of trashing all those good plans.

"I don't know," she said.

"Call them," he prompted. "How am I going to buy a car without you?"

She laughed again, and he loved the sound of it. "How are you even going to drive?" she asked.

"I can drive," he said indignantly. "It's just that I faint sometimes . . . Come on, I do not. I don't drive because I don't have a car anymore. *Call* them."

"Okay," she said. He sighed with relief. "On one condition, You come in here and help me make pancakes for Miri. I *promised.*"

"I don't know," he said warily. "Do you make your own syrup?"

"Mrs. Butterworth," she told him.

"Okay." He took his hands off the gate, and she lifted the latch from inside.

"You want to tell me where you've *been*, please?" Courtney asked. Sidney had just come in the front door.

"Hello," he said brightly. "How ya' doin', Susan?" he said, giving her a little wave. He went over to the bookshelf. "When I called, I told you I'd be home late," he said.

"You called me at eight o'clock this morning, Sid. Now, I'm serious. I've been worried about you all day." Courtney folded her arms and sat on the arm of the couch, glaring at him.

Sidney pulled a book off of the shelf. "I'm sorry," he said, pausing just long enough to let her know that he meant it, and he headed for the door again.

"Just hold it," Courtney said.

Calvin came in through the door. "There's a brand new Honda Prelude out there in the driveway," he said. "With a girl in it."

"It's mine," Sidney told him.

"You're kidding," Susan said. She went into the kitchen where she could see it from the window.

"You bought a car today?" Courtney asked him.

"Yes, m'dear. And I got a beautiful deal on it, too. See you." He kissed her, then he was out on the porch, heading for the car.

"Wait," Courtney called, chasing him out. "Where are you going? And who *is* that?"

"Ginny and I are going up to Miri's to read," he called over his shoulder.

Courtney stood on the porch for a moment, watching him go. She returned Virginia's wave, and then she followed Calvin into the kitchen saying, "I'm not sure I want to be a mother."

"Cheer up," Calvin said, putting both arms around her. "It could be worse. *You* could be supporting *him*."

"French braids, khaki pants, Hawaiian shirt, espadrilles, African jewelry, no hips, and more everything else than I've got," Susan was muttering. She was leaning across the sink, and she had her chin resting on her hands.

"What are you saying?" Courtney asked her.

Susan sighed. "And I *love* red cars." She turned around and regarded Courtney with a sort of wistful regret. "You know how long I waited for him?" She turned back to the window. "That Ginny," she said. "Why can't I look like that?"

"You do," Courtney said. "All the time."

"Yeah. But I'm not that *nice*," Susan sighed. "I suppose he took *The Princess Bride* with him?"

"I think that was the book," Courtney said. Calvin had found some cold chicken. "So what?"

Susan sighed again. "It's got to be serious."

Twenty-four

"Howdy," Sidney said as he stood in the doorway of the control room.

"Oh, man!" C.J. said, intercepting him. "Chris is _on_ one. Just keep a low profile and pretend you got here ten minutes ago."

"Panda disappeared on him," Graham explained from behind the console. He was sitting at the producer's desk next to Cap. "He spent the last week looking for her."

"Panda?" Sidney asked.

"Number four," Nee explained. "Regrettable."

"So, where is he?" Sid asked, looking around cautiously.

"He's going to be back here in a minute," C.J. said. "And he's not going to want to cut that song we were working on yesterday."

"He wrote it for Panda," Sid guessed.

"You've got it," C.J. told him.

Sidney reached back for Ginny's hand. It was a lovely thing to have your hand filled up with someone else's. He pulled her forward into the room as he came in. The moment Graham saw her, he stood up, and then so did Cap and Nee and C.J.

"This is my friend, Ginny," he said, without thinking offering them the intimate name. C.J. let out an involuntary whistle. Nee grinned. "I hope you don't mind that I brought her," Sidney said.

"Not at all," Graham said.

"Chris will," Cap pointed out. He leveled a look at Ginny. "I don't know what Sidney's told you about this bunch, but don't expect much of a welcome from Chris."

"Actually," Nee said, flipping a pick against his thumb nail, "Chris is rather a barbarian. But she has that resilient look, Cap. She's here with Sidney, after all."

Ginny grinned back at Nee.

"You've been to the music store," Cap said to Sidney. "Isn't that your stack of keyboards out there? This is the man who didn't have a synthesizer to his name."

"They got it all here on time," Sidney said, pleased. "I bought all those nifty digital keyboards yesterday and I haven't got the faintest idea how to use any of them. I'm going to have to figure out the sequencer and the sampler tonight. You want to help?" he asked Ginny with a small, warm, private look. "Two years I'm gone and the world turns high tech."

"I'm going to sit down," Ginny said, giving his hand a parting squeeze. "Back here?" she asked Graham, indicating a chair in the far back of the room, out of the work area. He nodded.

Chris came in through the door. "Well, we're all here," he observed. "Let me see what you've got." He put his hand out for Sidney's manuscript.

"I don't think we're going to want to start with this one," Sidney told him, handing it over.

"It's garbage," Chris agreed glancing at the first line. He went behind the console and shoved the chart into the trash. "Who's this?" he asked, catching sight of Virginia.

"A friend of mine," Sidney said. There was a finality about the statement that didn't leave room for comment. Chris gave him a you-know-better look and then shrugged, saying. "What the—. So, what else have you got?"

"Whatever you want," Sidney said cheerfully. C.J. looked at him. Sidney grinned, doing the Groucho Marx eyebrows and flexing his fingers.

"Look *out*," C.J. announced. "The man is *hot*."

Graham tapped his pencil against the producer's desk. "You all there?" he inquired.

"One hundred and ten percent," Sidney told him. There was music bouncing all around inside of him, and he could hardly keep himself still.

"Let's make hay," C.J. said, and he went into the studio.

"We're going to have to replace that one," Sidney said, meaning the chart in the trash. "Would you like to hear Ginny's song? Didn't know you had one, did you?" he asked her over their heads.

"Let's hear it," Graham said, glancing at Chris. Chris's fires seemed to be burning a bit low.

"You want the ballad, or the R&B first?" Sidney was on his way to the piano.

"R&B," Nee told him. "Things have been a little bit slow around here." Chris followed them out into the studio.

"Okay," Sidney said, sliding open the big glass door into the piano booth. "You've got it." He sat down at the piano, wiggled himself down onto the bench, and started to knock out a get-down bass figure with his left hand.

"All right," Nee said. He put his headphones on and picked up his bass. He hit a string, played a riff, and stopped to adjust the sound a little bit.

"Am I going to need a chart for this?" C.J. was complaining. "Man, I hate it when you're in shape. Who puts chords together like that?" Sidney went through a couple of chord changes. "Is that the bridge?" C.J. was asking. "Somebody get me some paper!"

Chris sat glumly behind the big black octagonal pads of the Simmons drums in the drum booth. "Don't you have anything to drink?" they heard him asking.

"Not a thing beyond what you saw in the refrigerator," Cap told him via the talkback. "Does Sidney have his phones on?" Cap asked.

"Man, put your phones on," Nee said. Sidney picked up his headset and put it on.

"Okay, give me the chorus again here, Sidney. I want to get a good punchy piano sound." Cap's voice came over the headsets. "Do it," Sid said, his voice picked up by the piano mikes. "Let's go. Let's go," he said, vibrating on the piano bench.

"Slow down," Sid heard Graham say. "We've got all day."

"Let me play it through once all the way. Okay? All the way, Cap. Okay? So, we're in four—and one and two and three—" He started the bass figure again, and then he brought the right hand down with it, pounding away gleefully. "Nice, isn't it?" he said over his shoulder.

"Just play it," Chris directed, his voice faint and harsh in the headsets.

Sidney went through the whole tune, singing it for them, and the rest of them played along, making a few notes count here and there. When it was over, Sidney was sweating. "You want to do it?" he asked.

"I do," Graham said. "Chris?"

"We'll do it," Chris said without much enthusiasm. Sidney saw the studio door open, and Ginny came in. She made her way over the wires and around the amps to the drum booth. She had a can in her hands. She opened the door to the booth, and Sidney cringed, waiting for Chris to take her head off. But he barely heard the "thank you, dear" from Chris, and then Ginny had left.

"Then let me give you the chords," Sidney said. "Meanwhile, I'm going to have to figure out how to get the clavinet sound on my DX-7." He got up from the piano and took off the headsets. He grinned all over and said, "I love *doing* this." Then he started fiddling with his synthesizers.

The session went all day and into the evening, a very intense and totally satisfying passage of time for Sidney, at least. They had a hard time keeping up with him, just as in the old days. The only problem was going to be getting into the technology, but he found he had a feel for that, and it didn't worry him much. Keyboard players like bells and whistles as much as anybody.

Ginny held her own, too, doing her job just as if she'd been born to it; she singled out Chris and worked at him until she had him talking. They'd spent the entire lunch together, Chris talking, Ginny listening. C.J.'d said, "He'll have *her* for lunch before he's through with her," but Sidney didn't think so. He was beginning to get a feel for her, and he thought she could probably take care of herself and Chris at the same time.

By the time they were ready to go home, Sidney was exhausted and exultant, Graham was pleased to death, and Chris was following Ginny around like a big sad dog. Sidney was having a hard time coming down enough to trust himself driving. "Man, you might as well be on drugs," C.J. told him on the way out. C.J. slapped Graham on the shoulder. "Let's get out of here before Sidney knocks the building down."

Sid finally had to intercede for himself with Chris, explaining that he needed Ginny to come and drive him home, now. "Bring her anytime you want," Chris told him, and he kissed Ginny's hand before he left.

"Girl, I think you're magic," Sid said as they walked out to the car. "I've never seen that old lion so docile."

"Oh, he's a nice man," Ginny said. "He just doesn't want to pay the price, that's all."

"For what?" Sidney asked.

"For anything. Anything can work if you're willing to make it work. But it's going to cost you something, and you've got to be willing to pay. If you don't pay, it won't work. Period. Unless you marry a saint."

"I'll pay," Sidney said, putting his arm around her. "How about dinner?"

"As long as you don't eat anything with sugar in it," she said, poking him.

Later, after a long, eventually calm dinner, they drove home along the coast. Ginny was quiet, her head back against the seat and her eyes closed.

"Did you have a good time?" he asked her quietly.

She opened her eyes. "Yes," she said. She turned sleepily and smiled at him. "Not as good a time as you did." She looked out of her window, and then she looked at him again. "I think Miri was right about you," she said.

He laughed. "Miri's going to kill me."

Her eyes were laughing with him. "Why?" she asked.

"Because now that I've got my brain working again, I couldn't give a hoot in Hades about technique."

"You're right," she said. "She's going to kill you."

"But there are other things of hers I care about," he said lightly.

She put her head back again and closed her eyes. "Watch yourself," she said.

Twenty-five

"You can't be serious," Chris said. "No way in this world am I going to play for some—" he broke off abruptly, "for a _church social._ He's kidding, isn't he?"

"I'm serious," Sid said. Cap was just seating himself behind the console, having taken a break of his own. Sidney answered Cap's inquiring eyebrow. "They're having this regional dance thing for the Single Adults, and they put me in charge of the music. _I_ don't know any bands. Look," he said to Chris, "Nee will do it. Graham will do it. C.J. will do it . . ."

"Of course C.J.'s going to do it," Chris said with disgust.

"You got a sound man?" Cap asked. He had his hands down inside the console, and there were electronics everywhere. Nee was sitting in the corner, alternately sipping at a Hansen's Natural Grapefruit and grinning hugely. Graham was sitting back in his chair, maintaining a ghost of a smile.

"What are you _doing_?" Sidney asked Cap.

"Oh, when Hodges was in here last night, he spilled a Coke on the console. I've got to get somebody in here to look at it. Something's fried. If you need a sound man, I'll do it."

"You mean it? Oh, that'd be excellent," Sidney said. "I mean, it's not like we can get Eddie Klien to do it."

"No, but you'll ask _me_," Chris said.

"Eddie's _union_," Sidney pointed out. Chris threw up his hands.

"Soloman, I'm not going to play a dance gig," Chris said, sitting back in his chair as if he'd said all he was going to say.

"Look," Sidney argued, "we've got to go over the tunes anyway. I mean, we've got an excellent chance here to see if they _work._"

"Come on, Chris," Cap said, fiddling around with something on the outboard rack. "Here you've got a real shot at the grass roots—really communicating with the common people. What else do you do the music *for*?"

"Money," Chris snorted.

"Come on," Sidney said. "There's seven hundred bucks in this."

There was a rich shout of laughter from Nee, who subsided immediately. "You can have my cut," he told Chris.

"Sidney," Chris said, very reasonable now, very rational. "We *can't* play a dance. We don't do copy work."

"Sure we do," Graham said, leaning forward, reaching for a pencil. He procured one and sat back in his chair again, crossing one leg broadly over the other. He was resting an elbow on each arm of the chair, holding the pencil in front of his face horizontally, one end in each hand. "Or we *should* be able to, don't you think? Sid can get us up some charts if we need them. Which we shouldn't."

"I don't do Air Supply," Chris said.

"Fine," Sidney agreed. "They don't do us, either."

"How many people know what you've got in mind?" Chris wanted to know. "Because if there's one person at that social who knows who we are . . ."

"Just Ginny," Sid said, holding up both hands.

Chris grunted.

"And it's not like anybody's going to recognize you. You just wear shades and a hat or something. Nobody ever looks at the drummer. Nee's the only one we're going to have a hard time camouflaging."

"Nobody ever looks at the bass player," Nee said.

They were all looking at Chris. He threw up his hands again helplessly. "I don't know how I ever got mixed up with you people," he said.

"You're going to do it?" C.J. asked.

"If you ever—*ever*—ask me to do something stupid like this again . . ." Chris said, pointing a finger at Sidney. But he couldn't finish what he was going to say. He just sat back in the chair, sighing with resignation. "Whatever you say," he said.

He left soon after that, as did Nee and C.J. It had been a long, hard day in the studio.

"You wouldn't think there was that much work to making music," Graham reflected, still sitting there with his pencil like a false horizon across his nose.

"I don't mind it," C.J. said.

"I don't either," Cap said. They both looked at him. "Well," he said, "I may be getting paid for it, but I'm still *working*."

Graham smiled to himself. "That was some little girl you brought in here Saturday," Graham said. "You'd better watch out, or Chris is going to steal her away."

"Not that girl," Sidney said. "*That* girl is something I never thought would happen to me."

"So she's a good one," Cap said. "She was awfully quiet the other day, but she had a good spirit about her."

"She calms my soul," Sidney said.

The control room door opened and Emily came in, very pretty and pink cheeked. She handed Cap a pile of papers. "Deena Anders called," she told him. Nobody had said a word. "Good session?" she asked.

"Real good," Graham said, looking at Sidney.

"That's good," Emily said, and she left the room, the air scintillating with indifference in her wake.

"You've got yourself a problem," Cap said.

"Don't I know it?" Sidney agreed.

Twenty-six

It was a strange thing, and he couldn't help reflecting on it as he rested on the couch in Miri's parlor, adrift in the heavy summer scents of her garden and in the delicate and fading light of the summer evening. He could remember coming to this house and sitting on this very couch as Miri's home teacher so long ago. This had been an unfamiliar place to him then, old-fashioned and formal. Now it was so integrated into the pleasant business of his life that it seemed like home to him.

Ginny came in. She had tiny little braids in her hair at the temples, holding the hair away from her gentle face. Looking at her was one of the purest pleasures of his young life. She leaned across him, reaching up under the lamp shade just beyond his head, and the light she loosed cascaded down over the couch and onto the floor. She sat down where it had pooled, close to the couch, just within reach. She opened the book she was holding and rested it on her lap.

She leaned back against the couch and sighed. "You're glad we're not at my house," he said, dropping his hand gently down on her hair.

"There aren't any synthesizers here," she agreed.

"It's taken me the last week just to figure out the sequencer," he said.

"Don't think about it now," she said. She turned around and got up on her knees, smiling. "Pleeeeese," she pleaded.

"Do you mind, really?" he asked, studying her eyes. "Do you mind that I spend so much time on the music?"

"No," she said. She took his hand companionably. "I just wanted to read you this book. It's okay to want a break, isn't it? Or do musicians never rest?"

"It depends on the diversion," he said. "You'd better read."

She turned around and sat down again, picking up the book and settling it in her hands. She was reading him her favorite book, *The Dean's Watch*, as an offering to him of herself, and he was enjoying it with all his soul. The book was quiet and warm, as she seemed to him to be, and full of compassion—which was like her, too. She read very well. He lost himself in the words for a time, and then he was outside of them again, thinking about her.

"I love you, you know," he said, stroking her hair. She stopped reading.

"You've been in love before," she reminded him.

"Hey," he said, giving her hair a gentle yank. He sat up and made her turn around so he could look at her face. "I'm going to be very frank with you, Gin. I've been in love *once*. Well, twice. And that's it."

"You're not in love with them anymore," she pointed out.

He put his hands in his lap, and he began to try to understand it himself. "The first time," he said, "it was with a tall, dark-haired, winsome young thing, name of Tricia. She was a singer, and I met her up in Utah at a ski resort. I was nineteen and she was another man's wife, and that was that. I never really knew her past saying a few words to her and listening to her sing. It wasn't what you'd call a love affair."

He sat back against the couch. "And then there was Emily. You know, she warned me at the time that I wasn't thinking very well. She was afraid that I joined the Church because I loved her. But I think what happened was that I thought I loved her because of the church I saw in her. She never did really get involved with me. She wrote. But we didn't really get to know each other as people much. There's your story about Emily. That was years ago. And then," he confessed, remembering it with chagrin, "I did fall in love with my day nurse at the hospital. But you probably know how that goes."

She smiled to herself. "I know," she said.

"Were you ever in love?" he asked. Her smile grew deeper and more private, and her cheeks flushed.

"A couple of times." She fiddled with the cover of the book, and he was instantly horribly jealous.

"Were they mistakes?" he asked. She looked up at him then, and there was a little sadness in her eyes.

"No," she said. "Just the wrong time. A couple of them were mistakes, I guess. Misperceived people." She put her hand on his knee. "How do I know," she asked, invoking whatever measure of wisdom he had, "that I'm not misperceiving you?"

"Does it matter to you?" he asked, very aware that his first confession hadn't been answered.

"Right now," she said, "it matters to me very much."

That's when he kissed her. It was something he could no longer help, or at least didn't really want to, and he was praying she wouldn't mind. He had his hands cradling her face, and he made no apology about it.

When he drew away, still embracing her with his eyes, he found her crying, and it wrung his heart with guilt. He wiped at the tears with his finger tips, whispering "I'm sorry" over and over again until she buried her face against his knee and refused to listen. He reached under her chin and made her turn her face up again. She stood up and went out of the room, and he sat there as awkward and stupid as he had ever felt in his life, until she came back in with a box of Kleenex and sat down again beside his knee, laughing a little ruefully.

She lifted the Kleenex box. "Beyond the sublime, there's always reality," she said, sniffling. He didn't know how to respond.

"I'm sorry," she said. She was twisting a Kleenex around her fingers. When she finally looked up at him, she had composed herself to a degree. "I don't have a lot of emotional resilience," she said. "My mother's death . . . ," here she did some more unhappy twisting, "took just about everything I had." She looked up at him again. "You . . . ," she shook her head at something she was thinking, "you may turn out to be way too much of an investment for me."

He didn't understand.

"I can't afford," she explained, "to feel the way I feel about you."

"Which is . . . ," he prompted.

The tears were still running in tiny bright lines from the corners of her eyes, and she dabbed at them with the shreds of her Kleenex. He leaned over and pulled a new one out of the box, tenderly prying the old one out of her hand.

"Thank you," she said. "See, I love you, too." She started to cry again.

"And that's a sad thing?" he asked.

"Sooner or later," she said.

"Why?" he asked, lifting her chin again. "We can't love each other? We can't stay together? What if I said I wanted to marry you?"

"How could you say that?" she protested. "You don't know me any better than you did the others."

"Yes, I do. How could I not know you? You're just wide open, Gin. Everything you are is right there on the outside for me. I could have known Emily fifty years and still never known a thing about the way she felt or the way she thought, because she made herself so closed off and private. You're not like that. I don't think you've been hiding from me."

"How do you know?" she asked.

"Because I just know. I think I can see you pretty clearly, and I *like* you. And I want to kiss you all over your face." He chucked her under the chin gently. "If I were going to pick somebody to be the other half of me, I'd pick Courtney. Or I'd pick you. There are advantages to picking you, see."

"But what if I yell at you for leaving your socks around?" she asked.

"Would you?" he wondered.

"I don't *know*. Do you leave your socks around?"

"I don't know," he said, considering. "Probably. Is that what's important?"

"Yes," she said. "That's what a marriage is — the little crummy everyday things you have to do over and over, and if you can stand picking up each other's socks all the time. I don't know how many people I've talked to who started out *in love* and ended up *hating* the other person's socks. Sooner or later, the socks get important."

"You told me," he said, "anything could work if you're willing to pay the price."

"How do you know if you can pay it, if you don't know what it costs?" she asked him. At first, he couldn't answer her.

Then he said, "You can be willing to try."

She put the side of her face against his knee, and they were quiet for a time.

"Is there something that you couldn't give up—not for anything?" she asked. She sat up and looked at him very soberly, her hand on his knee.

He nodded. "My principles," he said. "And the music."

"And your principles are . . . ," she said.

"Just the usual—the laws of God. And not asking directions no matter how lost I get." He grinned at her, and it put a dent in her seriousness. "And you?" he asked. "What couldn't you give up?"

"My*self*," she whispered fiercely. "My right to *be*." He was surprised at her intensity.

"Would picking up my socks damage that?" he asked.

"Yes," she said. "If you expected me to do it. And I know I would really hate it if you never picked up mine." She dared him to misunderstand. "Okay, I'm sorry if it sounds selfish," she said. "But I know that's how I feel, and it wouldn't help us at all if I whitewashed it. I don't want to disappear, do you understand what I mean?"

"Ginny," he said, "do you think, after I've been around Courtney and Susan, that I have any ideas at all about *expecting* anything out of anybody? If it even *seems* like I'm expecting some nice little traditional thing out of those two, they kick me around the house. But I like that. I like it that they're intelligent, independent people. It's not like *I* can carry anybody else, Ginny. If you need somebody who's going to be picking up your emotional socks all the time, I'm not the right person. Music is my life. It consumes my time. It's a passion with me. You know what it's been like this week. This is what it's *always* like. Just like this week."

She rested her chin on the hand that lay on his knee. "Could you pick up my emotional socks *some* of the time?" she asked.

He laughed and then kissed the top of her head. "How do you know you wouldn't get tired of me?" she wondered.

"How do you know you wouldn't get tired of me?" he responded. "I think everybody probably gets tired of everybody once in a while. I just know I love you. And I want to love you. And I do love you. I think it's worth the investment. I've got as much to lose as you do, Ginny. I believe it'll be worth it. You want to try? We could just pick a direction and go with it and see what we find out."

"What if *one* of us finds out it won't work?" she asked.

"Then we'll be kind. Don't be so scared. Nothing ventured . . ." He tapped her nose. "Grow old with me, will you? I asked Courtney to, but she won't. But you could."

"Let's make a deal," she said. "If I say 'yes, let's give it a try,' will you promise to go ahead and take me for granted as much as you're going to twenty years from now, so I know what I'm dealing with here? Don't be on your best behavior. Drop all the socks you have to drop. Treat me just the way you treat your sister. Will you do it?"

He smiled. "Just the way I treat my sister?" he asked. Her cheeks flushed again, and he thought it was awfully unfair of her. "Do we get to hold hands too?" he asked quietly.

The look she gave him was so modest and shy that it nearly did him in. He got down on the floor so that they were eye to eye, and he kissed her again until she had put her arms around his neck and he knew she had accepted his offerings, too.

"You'd better go," she whispered when he had finished, but her arms were still holding him, and he would much rather have yielded to them than to good sense.

"I'd better go," he echoed. They stood up, and she walked him to the door. "Will you change your mind tomorrow?" he asked, taking both of her hands in his as he stood on the cold side of her threshold.

"I don't know," she said grinning at him. "We'll have to wait and see. It's going to depend a lot on the color of your socks."

_____ *Twenty-seven*

The thing about dances, Emily thought for the fiftieth time in her life, standing back against the wall of the cultural hall with a plastic cup of punch in her hand, *is that they are always so* loud. She hadn't expected it to be like that tonight, not with this band, not with Cap sitting at the back of the hall behind the P.A. board. She'd said something about it to him, and he'd laughed. "You want it to sound like a dance, don't you?" he said. "Or else, what would the bishops have to complain about?"

At least, given how loud it was, the band sounded good. Of course, there were differing opinions about that. Part of the fun of being here tonight was circulating around and listening to the comments. Some people thought the band was fantastic; some thought it was only so-so. She'd heard somebody complain that the music was too rowdy, and then somebody else said that there were too many slow songs. Some people liked the copy tunes and hated the originals. Some people liked the originals and thought the copy tunes were hurting. The best one she'd heard back by the refreshments—it was right in the middle of "Can't See It," one of the band's own Top 40 hits of two years ago. Some callow male person had said that he just couldn't stand the way this band was butchering the song. It had been hard not to hit him with the truth.

She had danced a couple of times. Most of the guys—and there had been a respectable enough number—had left her alone once she got them to understand she was with the band. And she *was* with the band. Even if she couldn't really claim Sidney, there was always C.J.

Kinsey was here, too, somewhere. Emily was sure of that

because they'd come to the dance together, she and her sister. And Emily thought she'd seen Sidney's sister. Emily herself hadn't really wanted to come tonight.

Well, she had. But her dignity would have suffered a whole lot less if Sidney had just called her, or even if he'd mentioned the dance to her at the studio. He was always friendly at the studio. He always stopped to talk to her. But it was always such light talk, and that look of quiet interest he'd always had—that earnestness—it was gone now. And that made her worse than scared.

It was as she'd said to Kinsey—she'd spent two whole years writing to him, being as open as she could be short of making what would have been really unrealistic commitments. And his letters had been, if anything, more intimate than hers. So, what was she supposed to expect? That he shouldn't call her for a month? That they should start something really nice in the hospital, and that he'd let it die? There had to be a reason. There had to be reasons.

And when she'd walked through the door tonight, and she'd seen him up there—he looked just the way she'd always remembered him, the white pants and the Pierre Cardin jacket and the boat shoes—she hadn't expected it to hit her as hard as it had. She loved him still, and tonight it was a sharp pain inside of her.

Graham was up there on stage now, telling everybody that the band was going to take a fifteen-minute break. Emily pushed herself away from the wall and began to move up towards the stage. C.J. was crouched at the edge of it, talking down to Kinsey. Nee had disappeared. Graham had been cornered by somebody down on the floor. There was some girl talking to Chris. Sidney was still at the piano, playing something quiet, all alone.

Emily stopped where she was, just short of being close, watching him play. He really was good. It came to him so easily, playing like that. There was nothing that came that easily to her. Business. Some aspects of business were easy. But it was nothing like what he had. He could turn himself inside out, playing. This music was kind of quiet and sad, and she wondered if he was lonely. And then she wondered if maybe he had never really understood that she was finally *here.* Maybe he doesn't call me because he doesn't know I want him to. Maybe that's the reason.

The girl talking to Chris got up and left the stage. Chris didn't want to be there. He looked resigned and bored. Emily wished that Sidney would stop playing and come down. If he'd stop playing and come down to talk to C.J. and Kinsey, she could work her way in there, and things could go from there. But he didn't stop. And Emily's hands were shaking.

The girl was back on the stage again, handing Chris a cup and a napkin with food in it. Not a bad idea. Sidney would appreciate a gesture like that. Not a bad idea. Mentally she thanked the girl, hoping the girl wasn't going to get herself too involved with Chris. She was an extremely pleasant-looking person, and Emily felt a lot of sympathy for her. But then the girl got up, laughing, and patted Chris on the shoulder. She crossed the stage and stood behind Sidney for a moment as he played. Someone else had come up on stage from the other side, a younger girl, standing by the piano, talking to Sid. For a moment, Emily enjoyed a secret sort of pride. Those young women could stand there talking to Sidney, but she, Emily, *knew* him.

Emily looked at her watch. She wanted to go get the refreshments while she would still have time to talk, but something wouldn't let her leave, some little nagging discomfort.

The girl—the older one, the pretty one—said something, and Sidney turned, surprised. He hadn't known she was there. He smiled and reached back for her hand, which she gave him, and then he brought the hand to his cheek. Then he kissed it, all the time still playing with the other hand and talking to the younger girl. The older girl was close behind him now, obviously very comfortable.

Emily's stomach tightened up hard, and she suddenly felt a little weak at the knees. Maybe this was the reason. But Emily had never seen this girl before tonight. How could she be anything to him? Emily hadn't even seen her at the hospital. But then, she could have been just a stepsister, or an old friend . . .

Not true, of course. Anybody looking could tell that. This girl belonged to him. Emily's heart was pounding away inside of her chest, and she couldn't tell if she was mostly furious or hurt or embarrassed. She decided on furious. And she decided that something had to be wrong here with all of this. And she wanted to go home.

And then the break was over. Emily followed Kinsey across the hall and caught up with her back by the door. "Let's go home," she said.

Kinsey looked at her. "You saw that, I take it," Kinsey said.

"I saw it," Emily said. "And I want to go home."

Kinsey shook her head. "Emily," she said, "I'm not ready to go yet. I know you're probably hurt and angry, but I'm going to tell you this. I think you did it to yourself. I love you. But I told you all along—you couldn't expect him to hold still. His life had to keep going, and you didn't give him much to go on. You always told me you made a rational choice."

Emily felt the tears in her eyes before she knew she was going to cry. They were angry tears. "Thanks a lot," she said. It was the best she could do at the moment.

"Honey, I'm sorry. And I'd change it for you if I could. But you know as well as I do, you're both grown-up people, and you both have to deal with things as best you can. Emily, Sidney is wonderful, but he's a *musician.* I don't think you've ever understood that. I really don't think he would have made you happy. And like you said, you always knew this might be the price you had to pay for your schooling. Would you have given it up if you'd known this might really happen?"

"I know what I said. You don't have to throw back at me what I said. He could have *said* something. He could have called and *told* me."

"Emily, how could he have known it would matter to you?"

"Because he said he loved me." Emily was crying now, but she wasn't letting her face move. The tears were just coming down her face. She and Kinsey were standing near the wall in the shadow. It was still embarrassing.

"That was a long time ago," Kinsey said, "and I think, if you had really loved him, things might have been different. I think you're just scared. And you don't need to be. There are a thousand things waiting for you in your life. And there's going to be somebody who could make you happy. Sid's just not the one."

It was not the comfort Emily had been looking for. And Kinsey was not going to take her home. So Emily took herself outside and sat on the steps, just outside of the light. She could hear the band. Every time the door opened, the music swelled out and, almost as loud, the noise of the crowd.

She sat out there a long time in the warm air. There was a palm tree growing right by the door, and some Bird of Paradise. Emily wasn't focusing on anything very well.

And then there must have been another break, because someone was standing there beside her. A lot of people had been coming and going in the last few minutes, and the door behind her had opened and closed a hundred times. Now there was someone standing there on the stairs, right at her shoulder. At first she was scared. She looked up, and saw that it was Sidney.

She turned away, fixing her eyes on the base of the palm tree and composing her face so that he wouldn't see anything he shouldn't. She had no idea what she could say to him.

"I wanted you to meet Virginia," he said. "She wanted to meet you."

"I think maybe another time," Emily said. She had to clear her voice. He sat down on the step beside her.

"I should have called you, huh?" he said.

She shrugged, thinking, *It would have been nice.*

"I was going to. But I didn't know what I'd say. I didn't know what to do about you." He was looking at the palm tree too.

"I came out here to Los Angeles because of you," she said. It didn't sound like an accusation when she said it. Maybe it wasn't one.

"I didn't know that." He looked at her.

"You could have figured it out," she said. "And I did tell you. I tried to. I don't know, maybe I was too cool about it." She reached out and pulled a fiber off the trunk of the palm.

"Maybe you were," he said. "I'm sorry I didn't understand." He was quiet for a moment. "I think I'm probably going to marry Virginia," he said. From the way he said it Emily knew there wasn't actually much *probably* to it.

"You haven't known her very long." It was just a surmise, and it was, she knew, a fairly undignified way to be talking.

"Long enough," he said. "She's a good woman."

Emily threw the fiber back at the palm. "You can't know her very well, then," she said. It had been an immature and transparent thing to say. "I'm sorry. I don't know her at all. It's just, nobody's perfect."

"That's true," he said. He wasn't looking at her anymore. So she glanced at him. "I don't know what else to say to you, Emily," he said. "I want to say thanks for writing to me, and—for everything." *Like not introducing you to the Church? Like not calling you back, maybe? Go ahead, Sidney, think of something to thank me for.* "You took good care of the car for me," he said. "And thanks for coming to the hospital. And I'm sorry if . . ." He paused.

"It's okay," she said. "It just didn't work out the way I thought it would." *The way you made me think it would,* she couldn't help adding inside of herself. "I'm glad you're happy," she said. "And I'll come meet her sometime. But I don't think tonight. Okay?"

"Okay," he said. He sat there as if he wanted to say something else. She knew what he was thinking. He was thinking he didn't want to leave her sitting here unhappy. She thought, *If I were a better person, I'd lie to him and let him go away feeling like everything was just fine.* But she wasn't that good. It would take an angel to be that good.

"I guess I'd better go back in," he said. And then he said it again. "I'm sorry."

"It's not like my life is ruined," she said, trying to keep the sharpness out of the words. She shrugged again. "I'll get over it." But she kept telling herself, *Two years of my life.* And then she could hear Kinsey saying. "It's not like you *wasted* them." But she couldn't look up at him as he stood. In that moment she wanted to be part of him worse than anything she had ever wanted in her life.

"See you Monday," he said, and then he was gone, and so were all the other people who'd been standing around, because now the break was over and everybody else had gone back into the dance. Everybody but Emily. And then she realized the irony of it. For two years she'd disdained "activities" like this dance because she really hadn't needed them the way some women did. And now that's where she belonged, inside with the rest of the lonely people.

She put her hands over her face. Kinsey finally came out and gave her the car keys. "I'm going to go home with C.J.," Kinsey said. "I should have just given you these in the first place."

She sat there with the keys in her lap. And she told herself, *You might as well go on in and dance.* But she couldn't get around the bitterness at the center, so she picked up the keys, found the car, and went home.

Twenty-eight

The pie in Susan's hands was meant for Miri, but Susan left it sitting on the cottage porch when she saw that Virginia was alone in the back, because it was Virginia she had actually come to see.

She sat down next to the flower bed on which Virginia was working, and they exchanged the customary amenities, a trifle more awkwardly than usual as they had both relied on Courtney as their medium for so long.

The small talk ran out quickly. "You have something on your mind," Virginia said at last. Susan ran her fingers idly through the dense herbal border of the bed.

"You and Sidney," she started, having to squint slightly because the sun was slanting straight across the ocean into her eyes. "You have this sort of—" she waggled her hand in the air, meaning "more or less," though her very presence here gave more weight to the "more"—"air of togetherness about you lately."

"I guess we probably do," Virginia agreed.

"So," Susan said.

"We have an agreement," Virginia said. She wasn't hedging. She just wasn't sure what Susan wanted to know.

"Like, are there rings and things, yet?" Susan asked.

"No," Virginia said, pulling at a stubborn root. "Just raw commitment." She wiped her forehead with the back of her arm, and she smiled at Susan.

Susan nodded. "I wanted to explain to you . . . ," she began. "I wanted to apologize to you," she corrected herself. "If I've been a little distant, I want to apologize. See, I've known Sidney for a long time. And I guess I've always had kind of a little *thing* for him. I knew the second I saw you what you were going to end up doing to him. You're so much alike, you and Sidney." She put her hands in her lap and shrugged. "I couldn't help being a little jealous," she said.

Virginia sat, watching Susan. Her face was open and peaceful, and Susan felt no difficulty between them past what she was making for herself. "I wanted to tell you about him from my perspective," Susan went on. "So you'd know a little more. I mean, you'll know it all eventually anyway."

"I'd like to hear," Virginia said.

"And I want you to understand, I really do love Will. Will is a much better man for me than I think Sidney would be. But there'll always be something inside of me that loves Sidney." She looked up and said very quietly, "Sidney's the sweetest man I've ever known. He's been kind of a brat this summer, but all the other years I've ever known him, he's been even tempered and kind and just almost sickeningly honest. I think, after his mission, he was just so tired. And a little scared, probably." Susan smiled at Virginia.

"You're going to have to put up with the music. But he's not going to be a very hard man to live with. He's not the kind of person who leaves his shoes around the house. I've never even seen his living room messed up. Except for his desk. I've never really gotten that close to his bedroom, so I can't tell you very much about that."

Susan stood up. "I brought you and Miri a pie. I think you make a good pair, you and Sid. I just want you to understand what you've got."

Virginia stood up too, and she put her hand out for Susan's. Susan put her hand into Virginia's. "Thank you," Ginny said. Susan gave Virginia's hand a little squeeze, and then Virginia released her. Susan pointed at the pie. "See you, probably tonight?" And then she was gone. Ginny sat down in the grass and watched her go off down along the path. Then she smiled to herself and went back to her weeds.

Twenty-nine

"Just exactly what did you say to Mother in that last letter?" Courtney asked. She was sitting on the couch with a book in her lap. Sidney had just come in. He'd been running on the beach, and he was shining with sweat. It gave her a quiet, solid pleasure seeing him this way, so totally self-unaware again, a healthy young man, alive and glowing with the joy of it.

He wiped his neck with a towel and dropped into his chair, his cheeks all ruddy.

"What did you tell her?" Courtney asked again.

He sighed, trying to remember. "Okay—nothing." He stretched. "I told her I had another couple of weeks on the album, and that Ginny and I would come out for a visit after we were married. Except, I'm going to have to rearrange things now, because of the tour. And I told her that you are getting married in September, which you already told her. Why? I'm not in trouble again, am I? Did she call?"

"Yes," Courtney said, as if he shouldn't have had to ask.

"Oh, dear," he said. "So what did she say?"

"She's here." Courtney closed her book and gave him one of those when-will-you-learn looks.

"What?"

"She's *here*," she repeated, saying it very carefully so he couldn't help but understand.

"Where is she?" he asked, looking around as if he thought maybe she might be in the back bedroom.

"At the hotel," Courtney said. "Sidney, what did you expect? You just drop it on her that you're getting married. Did you even tell her when?"

"I don't *know* when."

"Well, you probably made it sound like it was going to be this *week*."

He was looking uncomfortable enough. "When is it going to be?" she asked.

"I don't know," he grumbled. And then he began to grin. "Another couple of weeks. Maybe a week and a half. It's not going to be any big deal. Just you guys and Miri and a few friends. So, it's not like we have a lot of plans to make."

"Okay, what are you going to do about Mother?"

"I don't know," he said, looking scared.

"Don't look at me," she said. "I'm not the one getting married in the Mormon temple. I don't have to explain anything. You should have written her after you did it."

"No," he said, "I couldn't do that."

"No," she agreed. "You couldn't."

He sighed again, putting his head down into his hands. And then he stood up. "I'm going to take a shower," he said. "You have her phone number?" Courtney pointed to the desk. "Okay," he said. "Okay." He looked at Courtney. "You know," he told her, "it would have been nice to have been pioneer stock."

She grinned at him. "We are," she said.

Claire sat stiffly in the right front seat of her son's new car. He'd made her wear the seat belt, and that hadn't helped her dignity any. She was not the one who had to talk; he was the one who had to talk. She was waiting for that. And she was going to try very hard to be receptive.

"So, Claire," he said, moving the car out into the traffic. "I don't think you're happy to be here."

She considered that. "I would have been happier of someone had invited me," she said.

He nodded.

She watched the low, green city go by her window.

"I didn't mean to make things hard for you, Mom," he said. He was trying to talk, trying to be honest. She tried to listen. "What I told you in the letter is true. We're just not going to make any big ceremony out of this. We just didn't want you to waste a trip."

"Being with my son when he's married would hardly be a wasted trip," she said. "And what about this girl's family?"

"Well, she doesn't really have any. Her parents are both dead." He turned up the on ramp to the freeway. It was lined with palm trees and some kind of dense green ground cover.

"I wanted to be here," she said. "You're my son."

"There's more to it, Mom," he said. "There's something I have to explain to you. I just have to know if you want to listen to me."

"Is it about your religion?" she asked, already feeling herself pulling away from whatever it was.

"Yes."

She looked out of the window some more, feeling that same tight fear in her chest she always felt when she thought about him and his religion. She looked at her son, bright and healthy looking now, different than last time she had seen him. Handsome. And he was respected in his business.

"If this is something that you really believe," she said, not sure yet if she meant it, "then I'll listen. But not to be convinced. Only to understand."

He nodded again. And then he started to get into the right lane. "I've got something I need to show you," he said. They were getting off the freeway. They drove through a neighborhood, along a small, quiet street—and then there was a huge white building that was obviously some kind of religious building. It had a spire, and there was a figure on top. Sidney turned the car up a drive and went through some open gates. The place was crowded with cars.

He found a parking place. He stopped the car there and came around to help her out. She was waiting for him to explain. He took her arm and they began to walk. It was a beautiful place, the grounds were so nice. She was frightened of it, though. It was a huge building, but it wasn't a cathedral. *What does anybody need such a large building for?* she thought.

There was a bench by a busy fountain, and he offered it to her. She sat on it. There were a group of people standing on the steps not far away—a wedding party. A photographer was spreading the bride's train out, arranging it carefully on the broad granite steps.

"That's a pretty girl," Claire said. "An expensive dress," she added. Then she said, "So, obviously, this is where you want to get married to this girl?"

"I wish you wouldn't call her 'this girl,' Mama," he said. "It hurts me."

"I haven't met her," his mother reminded him.

"I know," he said. "You will, tonight. And I think you'll like her. I like her. I'm praying you'll like her."

She looked at him, pained by the tone of what he'd said last. She patted his hand. "Don't worry, Sidney. I'm just a frightened, confused old woman. It frightens me to have you so far away; I don't even know you. I'll like her. You should pray she'll like me."

He laughed a little. And she knew he had already done just that.

"So, explain," she said, even though she knew she didn't want to hear.

"So, yes," he said, "this is where I want to marry her. This is the temple. This is the only place I want to be married." He looked down at his hands, then up at the building.

"And so?" she said.

He took a deep breath. "This is a very sacred place," he said, almost as if he were telling himself. "The most sacred place. In this place, people are sealed together—you know, the way it talks about in the Bible, how Peter had the power to seal on earth and in heaven? In there, they use that power, and they seal people together before God, for all time. Even after they die, they're sealed. It's more than just being married." He looked at her.

"And you think, after I die, I won't be married anymore?"

"You were married until death, Mama. That's what the words said." It was obviously not making him happy, talking about these things.

"And?" she said. This was obviously not *the* part. He was still getting to that.

"And nobody can go in there unless they really believe it is what it is. Unless they live their lives so that their lives say they believe it's that." He was still looking at her.

"So what you're telling me is that I can't go in there, and that's where you're going to be married."

"That's what I'm telling you," he said. And it was very difficult for her to understand.

"They would keep a mother from being with her son?" she asked. "What kind of a religion would separate a family? And you would let them do that?"

"No," he said. "*They* don't do that. *We* do that. *We*—you and I—we believe different things. I believe that the temple is the house of God. And I'd do anything so that I could go in there. To you, it's a building."

"So, you are choosing, then, between me—and what?"

"Between having you at the marriage, and being sealed to Ginny forever. Being sealed to my children forever. Never losing them. That's what I'm choosing."

"And because I can't go in there, then you and I will lose each other. Is that what you believe?"

"Yes. That's what I believe. Why do you think I always want to talk to you about it, Mother? Because I love you." She looked at him and was shocked to see tears on his face. "Because I love you. And because I don't want to lose you. And because I believe these things . . . ," he moved his arm indicating the building and whatever it stood for, *"so much."* He put his hands in his lap. "If you would let me tell you once what I believe, you wouldn't be so afraid of me."

But she was afraid. "You love me," she said.

"I do," he said.

"And this means so much to you."

"It does."

"And it means to you, keeping your family together."

"Yes."

She looked up at the building. "That's important to me, too," she said. "Keeping the family together."

"I know," he said.

"But you don't believe it," she said.

"Yes, I do. Why do you say that?"

"How could you?" she asked, surprising herself that she could say these things. "You know you must have asked yourself a thousand times, why did she let our family fall apart?"

He was quiet. She looked at him and there was deep pain on his face. He nodded. "When I was younger," he said. "But I understand more now."

"No," she said. She patted his knee. "I could have kept it from happening. I caused it myself. It was my doing."

"It takes two," Sidney said quietly. "That's what Dad says. It always takes two."

"Whatever," she said, brushing that aside with an impatience born of her own unhappiness at the memory. She took his face in her hand, and she spoke to him quietly and fiercely. "I'm going to tell you something. And I want you to listen. *Listen.* If you get married because you're looking for someone to take care of you, you will *never* be happy. Because *nothing* they do will ever be enough for you. You will always be disappointed, waiting, and they will hate you for it in the end. And you'll hate them.

"What you do is, you get married with the idea that you want to take care of someone else. Not smother them—take *care.* And then, you can always be satisfied. Because you can always be *listening* and loving and serving. There's always plenty of that you can do, and never have time to worry, are they watching out for me?

"And I'll tell you something else. I'm going to tell you what you, the man, should be worrying about—I know, because it's what I've been worrying about every married day of my life—it's not *your* life your girl is joining. You join your *two* lives together into a new one. Don't assume you're getting a servant and a cook and a bed partner. Don't assume *anything.* Every time that girl puts a meal in front of you or makes sure your clothes are clean or bears you a child, you think of it as a *favor.* She doesn't have to do that for you. And you treat her that way. And she'll take care of you. As long as she's the right girl."

She dropped her hand. It was shaking. She looked at the building again, and she hated it because she couldn't go in. "Why don't you take me back to the hotel?" she said. "And then maybe we can get Courtney and take her for lunch." She looked at her son. He was still looking at her, and on his face there was something she couldn't have named.

"I've been very selfish all my life, Sidney," she said. "I've always been very worried about myself. I'm surprised when you say you love me, because I don't see that there has been so much to love. Sometimes I think about you at night, and my heart aches to think about that face of yours when you were little." She stood up. "I would like to go, " she said.

She went home the next day. They told her she was welcome to stay, but she had a family to look after, and Sidney had been right after all about her being there. They took her to the airport, and they waited at the gate with her. She liked the girl. She was a bright girl, quick and independent. And she was kind; anybody could see that. The kindness went deep, too—not the kind that's assumed for the mother-in-law.

Now that Claire had been here, now that she had the girl's face in her mind, and she had seen Sidney looking like himself again, there wasn't much point in her staying. At least it hadn't been a wasted trip.

They called for the passengers to board, and she stood up. Sidney still had her hand luggage. "When you come out," she said to him, "I would like you to tell me what it is you believe about things. Not to be convinced. Just to understand."

He nodded, and there was that slow smile on his face that she loved so much. It was good to see him happy.

Claire turned to the girl and took her hand. "I want you to promise to be good to him," she said. "He's been bruised most of his life."

"I have not," he said.

"You have," she said, and she gave him the mother's look that kept him from contradicting further. "He's worth making happy," Claire said. "And I think you are, too." She patted the girl's hand, but she didn't hug her. It wasn't in Claire to hug. And then she nodded, picked up her luggage, and went to the door. After they had taken her boarding pass, she turned once more and saw them standing there together, watching her. They waved. She waved, too, thinking that they were a good couple, that they were lovely and young. And she was comforted inside.

_____ *Thirty*

One thing he had always loved about the beach at night was the strength of it, and the orderliness. The waves came welling in from miles out, rolling in to crest and foam and finally hurl themselves against the edges of the land, a mighty rush of noise and tumult and force that would expend itself so soon, and in the end, be nothing more than this gentle slap against the wet sand at his feet. And all this was done without his needing to understand. That the world could go on without his understanding was a great comfort.

He stood alone in the moonlight, a silvery web of music joining him to the tides, bathing himself in the peace of it after this fine and exhausting day. They had finished mixing the album last night. It had seemed like the end of an era, the last night of his old life.

Then the morning came singing, its million songs like sunlight. And early that morning there was a wedding—his own, though he wasn't sure he understood that so well, either. And then the luncheon with the band and the family and the friends. And then the afternoon spent moving one young woman out of his house and up into Miri's, while another was being moved out of Miri's and down into his house.

And his things, too, had been moved out of the little bedroom and into the one with the oak furniture in it. It had all been very strange. And so he had left the last little party, the last bit of moving and cleaning and putting things to rights, and he had come out to the sea, where things were now just as they had been the night before, and the night before.

He hadn't heard her coming up behind him. She slipped her arm around his waist, warm and familiar. Her touch had startled him at first. Then it had reminded him of other things. "Hello," she said. He put his arm around her.

"So, Courtney's all settled?" he asked.

"She is," his Ginny said, her voice quiet and rich against the night.

"And everybody's gone?" he asked.

"Every soul," she said.

He kissed her. He closed his eyes and he held her snugly against him and he put everything there was of him into that kiss, just the way he had ever wanted to do.

She sighed and she put her cheek against his shoulder.

"I guess we'd better go in," he said, mildly surprised at the huskiness of his voice.

She was grinning at him in the moonlight, young and fresh and so unguarded that he was suddenly afraid. He looked out over the ocean again, steadying himself. He had seen too much while he was growing up, and he knew things would not always be as sweet and easy as they were in this moment. He was afraid.

"What?" she asked.

He sighed, and then he rubbed his eyes. "I don't think I'm going to be able to get through the rest of my life without making mistakes," he said.

She laughed. "Me either," she said.

"Sooner or later I just know I'm going to end up doing something that hurts you. I never want to hurt you. I want life to be sweet for you."

"I'm not afraid," she said.

He tugged at the back of her hair thoughtfully. "By the way— I don't think I mentioned this before—I want twelve kids."

"Twelve kids," she murmured. "You're kidding, of course."

He smiled down at her.

"Tell me you're kidding," she said.

He laughed. And then he lifted his eyes and saw his house. He was still for a moment, and she turned to see what it was he was looking at.

"It's an old house," he said. "I wonder how many people have lived in it." She leaned against him.

The windows were alight and warm, and the house stood out

in the darkness like a small beacon. "There've been times," he said quietly, "when those windows were almost always dark. And that wasn't a bad thing, really. It was just because I was alone, and sometimes I liked it dark that way. But I think I like it better like this. Those windows with light in them. Like your eyes. They have light in them, too. I come out here in the dark, and I look back at the lights of my house—our house—" he looked down at her for a moment— "and I think there's someone in there, waiting for me to come back again."

He took her face in his hands. "Like your eyes," he said again. He could see her smiling at him, the light of his own windows reflected on her face, and he warmed himself in it. He patted her face.

"Ma'am," he said, offering her his arm, "let's go home."